Editor
Karen Tam Froloff

Editorial Project Manager
Lori Kamola, M.S. Ed.

Editor-in-Chief
Sharon Coan, M.S. Ed.

Illustrator
Howard Chaney

Cover Artist
Lesley Palmer

Art Coordinator
Denice Adorno

Imaging
Alfred Lau
James Edward Grace
Temo Parra

Product Manager
Phil Garcia

Publishers
Rachelle Cracchiolo, M.S. Ed.
Mary Dupuy Smith, M.S. Ed.

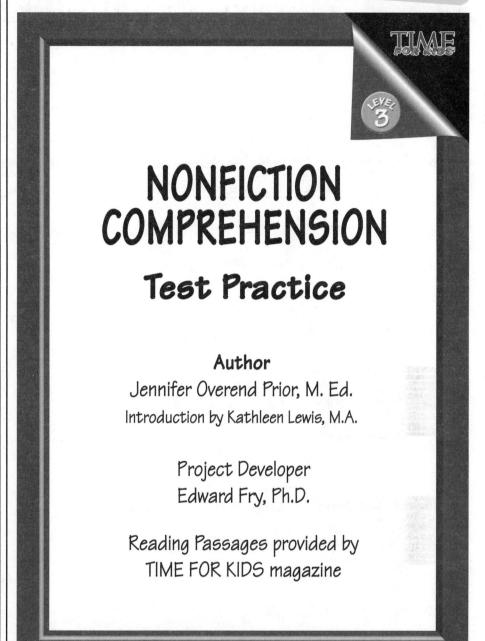

NONFICTION COMPREHENSION
Test Practice

Author
Jennifer Overend Prior, M. Ed.
Introduction by Kathleen Lewis, M.A.

Project Developer
Edward Fry, Ph.D.

Reading Passages provided by
TIME FOR KIDS magazine

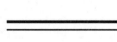

Teacher Created Materials, Inc.
6421 Industry Way
Westminster, CA 92683
www.teachercreated.com
ISBN-1-07439-3510-1
©2001 Teacher Created Materials, Inc.
Made in U.S.A.

Table of Contents

(**Note:** Each six-part lesson revolves around an article from *Time For Kids*. The article titles are listed here for you to choose topics that will appeal to your students, but the individual articles do not begin on the first page of the lessons. The lessons in this book may be done in any order.)

Introduction

Why Every Teacher Needs This Book

In a day of increased accountability and standards-based instruction, teachers are feeling greater pressure for their students to perform well on standardized tests. Every teacher knows that students who can read, and comprehend what they read, will have better test performance.

In many classrooms today, teachers experience challenges they are not trained to meet, including limited English speakers, students with disabilities, high student mobility rates, and student apathy. Many states with poor standardized test scores have students that come from print-poor environments. Teachers need help developing competent readers and students who can apply their knowledge in the standardized test setting.

The *Nonfiction Comprehension Test Practice* series is a tool that will help teachers to teach comprehension skills to their students and enable their students to perform better in a test setting. This series supplies motivating, readable, interesting, nonfiction text, and comprehension exercises to help students practice comprehension skills while truly becoming better readers. The activities can be quick or in depth, allowing students to practice skills daily. What is practiced daily will be acquired by students. Practice for standardized tests needs to be started at the beginning of the school year, not a few weeks before the tests. The articles in this series are current and develop knowledge about today's world as well as the past. Students will begin thinking, talking, and developing a framework of knowledge which is crucial for comprehension.

When a teacher sparks an interest in knowledge, students will become life-long learners. In the process of completing these test practice activities, not only will you improve your students' test scores, you will create better readers and life-long learners.

Readability

All of the articles used in this series have been edited for readability. The Fry Graph, The Dale-Chall Readability Formula, or the Spache Readability Formula was used depending on the level of the article. Of more than 100 predictive readability formulas, these are the most widely used. These formulas count and factor in three variables: the number of words, syllables, and sentences. The Dale-Chall and Spache formulas also use vocabulary lists. The Dale-Chall Formula is typically used for upper-elementary and secondary grade-level materials. It uses its own vocabulary list and takes into account the total number of words and sentences. The formula reliably gives the readability for the chosen text. The Spache Formula is vocabulary-based, paying close attention to the percentage of words not present in the formula's vocabulary list. This formula is best for evaluating primary and early elementary texts. Through the use of these formulas, the levels of the articles are appropriate and comprehensible for students at each grade level.

Introduction (cont.)

General Lesson Plan

At each grade level of this series, there are 20 articles that prove interesting and readable to students. Each article is followed by questions on the following topics:

Sentence comprehension—Five true/false statements are related back to one sentence from the text.

Word study—One word from the text is explained (origin, part of speech, unique meaning, etc.). Activities can include completion items (cloze statements), making illustrations, or compare and contrast items.

Paragraph comprehension—This section contains one paragraph from the text and five multiple-choice questions directly related to that paragraph. The questions range from drawing information directly from the page to forming opinions and using outside knowledge.

Whole story comprehension—Eight multiple-choice questions relate back to the whole article or a major part of it. They can include comprehension that is factual, is based on opinion, involves inference, uses background knowledge, involves sequencing or classifying, relates to cause and effect, and involves understanding the author's intent. All levels of reading comprehension are covered.

Enrichment for language mechanics and expression—This section develops language mechanics and expression through a variety of activities.

Graphic development—Graphic organizers that relate to the article are used to answer a variety of comprehension questions. In some lessons, students create their own maps, graphs, and diagrams that relate to the article.

The following is a list of words from the lessons that may be difficult for some students. These words are listed here so that you may review them with your students as needed.

Word	Page	Word	Page
tornado	19	conservation	75
exclamation	23	contraction	77
fantastic	27	Prospector	81
Shaman's Apprentice	33	Hartigan	87
Synonym	35	refrigerator	105
Titanosaur	52	cafeteria	111
Endurance	55	Yangtze	123
apostrophe	65	Tibet	129
Garissa	69	enjoyment	137

Introduction (cont.)

What Do Students Need to Learn?

Successful reading requires comprehension. Comprehending means having the ability to connect words and thoughts to knowledge already possessed. If you have little or no knowledge of a subject, it is difficult to comprehend an article or text written on that subject. Comprehension requires motivation and interest. Once your students start acquiring knowledge, they will want to fill in the gaps and learn more.

In order to help students be the best readers they can be, a teacher needs to be familiar with what students need to know to comprehend well. A teacher needs to know Bloom's levels of comprehension, traditional comprehension skills and expected products, and the types of questions that are generally used on standardized comprehension tests, as well as methods that can be used to help students to build a framework for comprehension.

Bloom's Taxonomy

In 1956, Benjamin Bloom created a classification for questions that are commonly used to demonstrate comprehension. These levels are listed here along with the corresponding skills that will demonstrate understanding and are important to remember when teaching comprehension to assure that students have attained higher levels of comprehension. Use this classification to form your own questions whenever students read or listen to literature.

Knowledge—Students will recall information. They will show knowledge of dates, events, places, and main ideas. Questions will include words such as: who, what, where, when, list, identify, and name.

Comprehension—Students will understand information. They will compare and contrast, order, categorize, and predict consequences. Questions will include words such as: compare, contrast, describe, summarize, predict, and estimate.

Application—Students will use information in new situations. Questions will include words such as: apply, demonstrate, solve, classify, and complete.

Analysis—Students will see patterns. They will be able to organize parts and figure out meaning. Questions will include words such as: order, explain, arrange, and analyze.

Synthesis—Students will use old ideas to create new ones. They will generalize, predict, and draw conclusions. Questions will include words such as: what if?, rewrite, rearrange, combine, create, and substitute.

Evaluation—Students will compare ideas and assess value. They will make choices and understand a subjective viewpoint. Questions will include words such as: assess, decide, and support your opinion.

Introduction (cont.)

Comprehension Skills

There are many skills that form the complex activity of comprehension. This wide range of understandings and abilities develops over time in competent readers. The following list includes many traditional skills found in scope and sequence charts and standards for reading comprehension.

identifies details

recognizes stated main idea

follows directions

determines sequence

recalls details

locates reference

recalls gist of story

labels parts

summarizes

recognizes anaphoric relationships

identifies time sequence

describes a character

retells story in own words

infers main idea

infers details

infers cause and effect

infers authors purpose/intent

classifies, places into categories

compares and contrasts

draws conclusions

makes generalizations

recognizes paragraph (text) organization

predicts outcome

recognizes hyperbole and exaggeration

experiences empathy for a character

experiences an emotional reaction to the text

judges quality/appeal of text

judges author's qualifications

recognizes facts vs. opinions

applies understanding to a new situation

recognizes literary style

recognizes figurative language

identifies mood

identifies plot and story line

Introduction (cont.)

Observable Comprehension Products

There are many exercises that students can complete when they comprehend the material they read. Some of these products can be performed orally in small groups. Some lend themselves more to independent paper-and-pencil type activities. Although there are more, the following are common and comprehensive products of comprehension.

Recognizing—underlining, multiple choice items, matching, true/false statements

Recalling—writing a short answer, filling in the blanks, flashcard question and answer

Paraphrasing—retelling in own words, summarizing

Classifying—grouping components, naming clusters, completing comparison tables, ordering components on a scale

Following directions—completing steps in a task, using a recipe, constructing

Visualizing—graphing, drawing a map, illustrating, making a time line, creating a flow chart

Fluent reading—accurate pronunciation, phrasing, intonation, dramatic qualities

Reading Comprehension Questions

Teaching the kinds of questions that appear on standardized tests gives students the framework to anticipate and thus look for the answers to questions while reading. This framework will not only help students' scores, but it will actually help them learn how to comprehend what they are reading. Some of the types of questions students will find on standardized comprehension tests are as follows:

Vocabulary—These questions are based on word meaning, common words, proper nouns, technical words, geographical words, and unusual adjectives.

Facts—These questions ask exactly what was written, using who, what, when, where, why, how, and how many.

Sequence—These questions are based on order—what happened first, last, and in between.

Conditionals—These questions use qualifying terms such as: if, could, alleged, etc.

Summarizing—These questions require students to restate, choose main ideas, conclude, and create a new title. Also important here is for students to understand and state the author's purpose.

Outcomes—These questions often involve readers drawing upon their own experiences or bringing outside knowledge to the composition. Students must understand cause and effect, results of actions, and implications.

Opinion—These questions ask the author's intent and mood and require use of background knowledge to answer.

Introduction *(cont.)*

Graphic Organizers

Reading and comprehension can be easier for students with a few simple practices. For top comprehension, students need a wide vocabulary, ideas about the subject they are reading, and understanding of the structure of the text. Pre-reading activities will help students in all of these areas. Graphic organizers help students build vocabulary, brainstorm ideas, and understand the structure of the text.

Graphic organizers aid students with vocabulary and comprehension. Graphic organizers can help students comprehend more and, in turn, gain insight into how to comprehend in future readings. This process teaches a student a way to connect new information to prior knowledge that is stored in his or her brain. Different types of graphic organizers are listed below by category.

Concept organizers include: semantic maps, spider maps (word webs), Venn diagrams, and fishbone diagrams.

Semantic map—This organizer builds vocabulary. A word for study is placed in the center of the page, and four categories are made around it. The categories expand on the nature of the word and relate it back to personal knowledge and experience of the students.

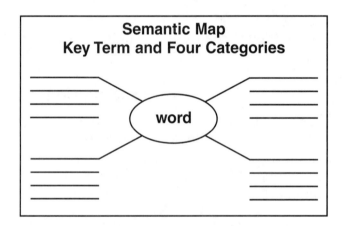

Spider map (word web)—The topic, concept, or theme is placed in the middle of the page. Like a spider's web, thoughts and ideas come out from the center, beginning with main ideas and flowing out to details.

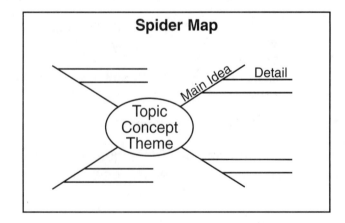

Introduction (cont.)

Venn diagram—This organizer compares and contrasts two ideas. With two large circles intersecting, each circle represents a different topic. The area of each circle that does not intersect is for ideas and concepts that are only true about one topic. The intersection is for ideas and concepts that are true about both topics.

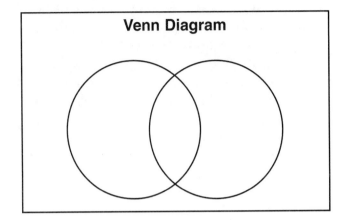

Fishbone diagram—This organizer deals with cause and effect. The result is listed first, branching out in a fishbone pattern with the causes that lead up to the result, along with other effects that happened along the way.

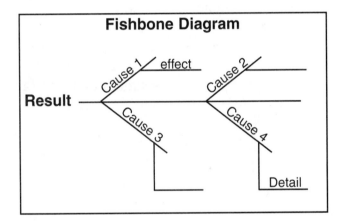

Continuum organizers can be linear or circular and contain a chain of events. These include time lines, chain of events, multiple linear maps, and circular or repeating maps.

Time lines—Whether graphing ancient history or the last hour, time lines help students to see how events have progressed and understand patterns in history.

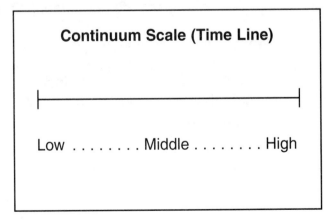

Introduction *(cont.)*

Chain of Events—This organizer not only shows the progression of time but also emphasizes cause and effect. Beginning with the initiating event inside of a box, subsequent arrows and boxes follow showing the events in order.

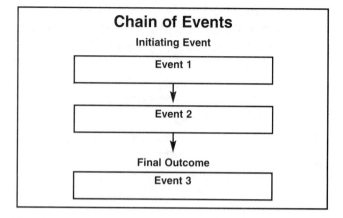

Multiple linear maps—These organizers can help students visualize how different events can be happening at the same time, either in history or in a story, and how those events affect each other.

Circular or repeating maps—These organizers lend themselves to events that happen in a repeating pattern like events in science, such as the water cycle.

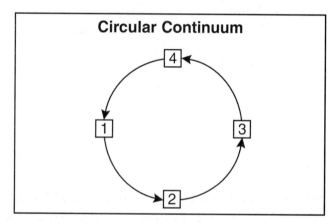

Hierarchical organizers show structure. These include: network trees, structured overviews, and class/example and properties maps. These organizers help students begin to visualize and comprehend hierarchy of knowledge, going from the big picture to the details.

Network tree—This organizer begins with a main, general topic. From there it branches out to examples of that topic, further branching out with more and more detail.

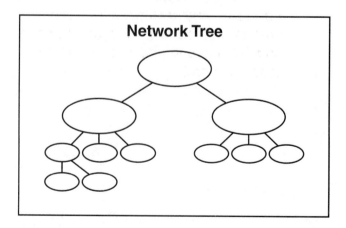

Introduction *(cont.)*

Structured overview—This is very similar to a network tree, but it varies in that it has a very structured look.

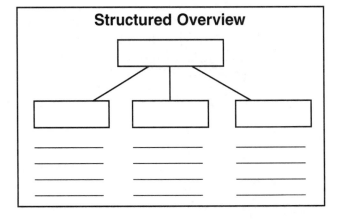

Class/example and properties map—Organized graphically, this map gives the information of class, example, and properties.

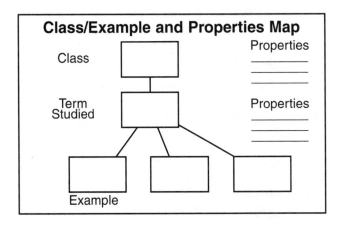

Spreadsheets are important organizers today. Much computer information is stored on spreadsheets. It is important for students to learn how to create, read, and comprehend these organizers. These include semantic feature analysis, compare and contrast matrices, and simple spreadsheet tables.

Semantic feature analysis—This organizer gives examples of a topic and lists features. A plus or a minus indicates if that example possesses those features.

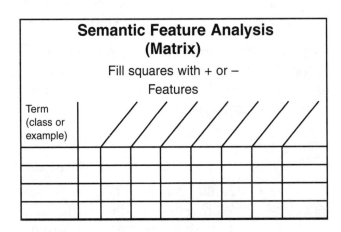

Introduction (cont.)

Graphic Organizers (cont.)

Compare and contrast matrix—This organizer compares and contrasts two or more examples on different attributes.

Compare/Contrast Matrix (Spreadsheets)		
Attribute 1		
Attribute 2		
Attribute 3		

Simple spreadsheet table—Much information can be visualized through spreadsheets or tables. Choose examples and qualities and arrange them in spreadsheet style.

Maps are helpful in understanding spatial relationships. There are geographical maps, but there are also street maps and floor plans.

Geographical map—These organizers can range from globes to cities and details are limited.

Street map—Information on this type of organizer becomes more detailed.

Floor plan—This organizer becomes more detailed, from a building to a room or a student's desk.

Numerical graphs such as bar graphs, pie charts, and tables become important in comprehension, too.

Bar graph—With a vertical and a horizontal axis, this graph shows a comparison between subjects. It is important to be able to draw the correct information out of it.

Pie chart—In the circular shape of a pie, amounts totaling 100% are shown as pieces of pie. Once again, drawing correct information is important.

Using graphic organizers while reading class material will help students know what to do in order to better comprehend material on standardized comprehension tests. Further, a varied use of all types of organizers will help students of different learning styles hit a method that works for them.

Pre-reading Strategies

It is widely understood that for comprehension and acquisition to take place, new information must be integrated with what the reader knows. Pre-reading strategies will help students to build knowledge and restructure the information they already possess in order to more fully comprehend what they are reading. After a teacher has spent time teaching pre-reading strategies, students will know what to do when reading on their own.

Introduction *(cont.)*

Building Vocabulary

Common sense reveals that there is a symbiotic relationship between knowledge of vocabulary and comprehension. Vocabulary development and comprehension span the curriculum. Students come across a large and diverse vocabulary in science, social science, mathematics, art, and even physical education. Skills and strategies for understanding vocabulary can be taught throughout the day. You can build your students' vocabulary directly and/or indirectly. Both ways have shown merit for different learners, so a combination will be sure to help all of the learners in your classroom.

Whether done directly or indirectly, teaching the kind of vocabulary that occurs in a text will greatly improve comprehension. Teaching vocabulary directly, a teacher would list the vocabulary in the text and have the students find the definitions in some manner. Indirectly, a teacher would introduce the content of the text and then elicit vocabulary that the students bring with them on the subject. The use of graphic organizers is helpful in doing this. (See page 8 for different types.) The teacher would lead the discussion to specific words if necessary.

Direct teaching—The more conventional way of teaching vocabulary has its merits. Give students a list of vocabulary words and they look them up. This way teaches the use of reference materials and for some learners it is a good way to learn vocabulary. However, students truly learn vocabulary when they are involved in the construction of meaning rather than simply memorizing definitions.

Incidental or indirect teaching—This is really a combination of direct teaching and incidental learning for the well-equipped teacher. Teaching in this fashion, a teacher uses the students' knowledge and interests to begin a vocabulary development session that will end with what he or she wants the students to learn. Along the way, the teacher builds a grand vocabulary list and student interest. Also, students buy into the fact that they are part of the process and that learning vocabulary can be a personal experience that they can control. The students will learn how to become independent learners, studying things that interest them.

A general approach to building vocabulary could include the following:

Semantic association—Students brainstorm a list of words associated with a familiar word, sharing everyone's knowledge of vocabulary and discussing the less familiar words.

Semantic mapping—Once the brainstorming is done, students can group the words into categories, creating a visual organization to understand relationships.

Semantic feature analysis—Another way to group words is according to certain features. Use a chart to show similarities and differences between words.

Analogies—This practice will further help students to see the relationships of words. Also, analogies are often used on standardized tests. (e.g., Doctor is to patient as teacher is to ___student___.)

Word roots and origins—The study of these, as well as affixes, will help students to deduce new words. Students can ask themselves, "Does it look like a word I know? Can I figure out the meaning in the given context?"

Introduction (cont.)

Building Vocabulary (cont.)

Synonyms and antonyms—The study of these related words provides a structure for meaning and is also good practice for learning and building vocabulary.

Brainstorming—The use of graphic organizers to list and categorize ideas will help greatly with comprehension. A great way to get started is with a KWL chart. By listing ideas that are known, what students want to know, and, when finished, what they learned, relationships will be established so that comprehension and acquisition of knowledge will take place. Word webs work well, too. Anticipating the types of words and ideas that will appear in the text will help with fluency of reading as well as with comprehension.

Understanding Structure

To be able to make predictions and find information in writing, a student must understand structure. From the structure of a sentence to a paragraph to an essay, this skill is important and sometimes overlooked in instruction. Some students have been so immersed in literature that they have a natural understanding of structure. For instance, they know that a fairy tale starts out "Once upon a time . . . ," has a good guy and a bad guy, has a problem with a solution, and ends ". . . happily ever after." But when a student does not have this prior knowledge, making heads or tails of a fairy tale is difficult. The same holds true with not understanding that the first sentence of a paragraph will probably contain the main idea, followed with examples of that idea. When looking back at a piece to find the answer to a question, understanding structure will allow students to quickly scan the text for the correct area in which to find the information. Furthermore, knowing where a text is going to go structurally will help prediction as well as comprehension.

Building a large vocabulary is important for comprehension, but comprehension and acquisition also require a framework for relating new information to what is already in the brain. Students must be taught the structure of sentences and paragraphs. Knowing the structure of these, they will begin to anticipate and predict what will come next. Not having to decode every word reduces the time spent reading a sentence and thus helps students remember what they read at the beginning of the sentence. Assessing an author's purpose and quickly recalling a graphic or framework of personal knowledge will help a reader predict and anticipate what vocabulary and ideas might come up in an article or story.

Several activities will help with understanding structure. The following list offers some ideas to help students:

Write—A great way to understand structure is to use it. Teach students the proper structure when they write.

Color code—When reading a text, students can use colored pencils or crayons to color code certain elements such as main idea, supporting sentences, and details. Once the colors are in place, they can study and tell in their own words about paragraph structure.

Introduction (cont.)

Understanding Structure (cont.)

Go back in the text—Discuss a comprehension question with students. Ask them, "What kinds of words are you going to look for in the text to find the answer? Where are you going to look for them?" (The students should pick main ideas in the question and look for those words in the topic sentences of the different paragraphs.)

Graphic organizers—Use the list of graphic organizers (page 8) to find one that will suit your text. Have students create an organizer as a class, in a small group, or with a partner.

Study common order—Students can also look for common orders. Types of orders can include chronological, serial, logical, functional, spatial, and hierarchical.

Standardized Tests

Standardized tests have taken a great importance in education today. As an educator, you know that standardized tests do not necessarily provide an accurate picture of a student. There are many factors that do not reflect the students' competence that sway the results of these tests.

- The diversity of our big country makes the tests difficult to norm.
- Students that are talented in areas other than math and language cannot show this talent.
- Students who do not speak and read English fluently will not do well on standardized tests.
- Students who live in poverty do not necessarily have the experiences necessary to comprehend the questions.

The list could go on, but there does have to be some sort of assessment of progress that a community can use to decide how the schools are doing. Standardized tests and their results are receiving more and more attention these days. The purpose of this series, along with creating better readers, is to help students get better results on standardized tests.

Test Success

The ability to do well when taking traditional standardized tests on comprehension requires at least three things:

- a large vocabulary of sight words
- the mastery of certain specific test-taking skills
- the ability to recognize and control stress

Vocabulary has already been discussed in detail. Test-taking skills and recognizing and controlling stress can be taught and will be discussed in this section.

Introduction *(cont.)*

Test-Taking Skills

Every student in your class needs good test-taking skills, and almost all of them will need to be taught these skills. Even fluent readers and extremely logical students will fair better on standardized tests if they are taught a few simple skills for taking tests.

These test-taking skills are:

- The ability to follow complicated and sometimes confusing directions. Teach students to break down the directions and translate them into easy, understandable words. Use this series to teach them the types of questions that will appear.

- The ability to scale back what they know and concentrate on just what is asked and what is contained in the text—show them how to restrict their responses. Question students on their answers when doing practice exercises and have them show where they found the answer in the text.

- The ability to rule out confusing distracters in multiple choice answers. Teach students to look for key words and match up the information from the text.

- The ability to maintain concentration during boring and tedious repetition. Use practice time to practice this and reward students for maintaining concentration. Explain to students why they are practicing and why their concentration is important for the day of the test.

There are also environmental elements that you can practice with throughout the year in order for your students to become more accustomed to them for the testing period.

If your desks are pushed together, have students move them apart so they will be accustomed to the feel on test-taking day.

- Put a "Testing—Do Not Disturb" sign on the door.

- Require "test etiquette" when practicing: no talking, attentive listening, and following directions.

- Provide a strip of construction paper for each student to use as a marker.

- Establish a routine for replacing broken pencils. Give each student two sharpened pencils and have a back-up supply ready. Tell students they will need to raise their broken pencil in their hand, and you will give them a new one. One thing students should not worry about is the teacher's reaction to a broken pencil.

- Read the instructions to the students as you would when giving a standardized test so they grow accustomed to your test-giving voice.

- As a teacher, you probably realize that what is practiced daily is what is best learned. All of these practices work well to help students improve their scores.

Introduction (cont.)

Reduce Stress and Build Confidence

As well as the physical and mental aspects of test-taking, there is also the psychological. It is important to reduce students' stress and increase students' confidence during the year.

- In order to reduce stress, it first needs to be recognized. Discuss feelings and apprehensions about testing. Give students some tools for handling stress.

- Begin talking about good habits at the beginning of the year. Talk about getting enough sleep, eating a good breakfast, and exercising before and after school. Consider sending home a letter encouraging parents to start these good routines with their children at home.

- Explain the power of positive thought to your students. Tell them to use their imaginations to visualize themselves doing well. Let them know that they have practiced all year and are ready for what is to come.

- Remember to let students stretch and walk around between tests. Try using "Simon Says" with younger students throughout the year to get them to breathe deeply, stretch, and relax so it won't be a novel idea during test time.

- Build confidence during the year when using the practice tests. Emphasize that these tests are for learning. If they could get all of the answers right the first time, they wouldn't need any practice. Encourage students to state at least one thing they learned from doing the practice test.

- Give credit for reasonable answers. Explain to students that the test makers write answers that seem almost true to really test the students' understanding. Encourage students to explain why they chose the answers they gave, and then reason with the whole class on how not to be duped the next time.

- Promote a relaxed, positive outlook on test-taking. Let your students know on the real day that they are fully prepared to do their best.

Introduction *(cont.)*

Suggestions for the Teacher

When practicing skills for comprehension, it is important to vocalize and discuss the process in finding an answer. After building vocabulary, tapping background knowledge, and discussing the structure that might be used in the article, have the students read the article. If they are not able to read the article independently, have them read with a partner or in a small teacher-lead group. After completing these steps, work through the comprehension questions. The following are suggestions for working through these activities.

- Have students read the text silently and answer the questions.

- Have students correct their own papers.

- Discuss each answer and how the students came to their answers.

- Refer to the exact wording in the text.

- Discuss whether students had to tap their own knowledge or not.

Answer Sheet

The teacher can choose to use the blank answer sheet located at the back of the book for practice filling in bubble forms for standardized tests. The rows have not been numbered so that the teacher can use the form for any test, filling in the numbers and copying for the class as necessary. The teacher can also have the students write the answers directly on the pages of the test practice sheets instead of using the bubble sheet.

Summary

Teachers need to find a way to blend test preparation with the process of learning and discovery. It is important for students to learn test-taking skills and strategies because they will be important throughout life. It is more important for students to build vocabulary and knowledge, to create frameworks for comprehension, and to become fluent readers.

The *Nonfiction Comprehension Test Practice* series is an outstanding program to start your students in the direction of becoming better readers and test-takers. These are skills they will need throughout life. Provide an atmosphere of the joy of learning and create a climate for curiosity within your classroom. With daily practice of comprehension skills and test-taking procedures, teaching comprehension may seem just a little bit easier.

Sentence Comprehension

Directions: Read the following sentences carefully and answer the questions below "True" (T) or "False" (F).

> I yelled, "Tornado!" It was so close that I could see tree limbs, doors, and all sorts of other stuff that this monster had swallowed.

1. The tornado turned into a real monster. _____

2. A car was seen inside the tornado. _____

3. The tornado was close by. _____

4. The tornado was carrying tree limbs. _____

5. The tornado has a mouth to swallow food. _____

Word Study

Directions: Read the definition. Then underline the words in the sentence that represent an example of personification.

> **personification**
>
> giving an object human qualities

My heart had moved up to my throat and was beating so hard I thought it would leap from my body.

Paragraph Comprehension

Directions: Read the paragraph below and answer the following questions.

Once we parked, we leapt from the car and lay pressed up against the concrete wall of the overpass. Before I could count to 20, a roaring surrounded us. It sounded like a freight train passing overhead. Then, suddenly, it was over. We had made it. Some trees were uprooted. Tree branches and flowers were scattered all over. Yet everything was calm and quiet.

---

1. They hid from the storm

   a. in the car.

   b. under a tree.

   c. under an overpass.

   d. underground.

2. The first sound they heard was

   a. a roaring sound.

   b. the breeze blowing.

   c. animals moving about.

   d. birds singing.

3. The tornado sounded like

   a. a freight train.

   b. a loud storm.

   c. wolves howling.

   d. a crowd of shouting people.

4. How long did the tornado last?

   a. many hours

   b. most of the day

   c. only a few minutes

   d. one hour

5. When the tornado left,

   a. it was still raining.

   b. the wind was still blowing.

   c. it was calm and quiet.

Whole Story Comprehension

Directions: Read the story below and answer the questions on the following page.

Racing a Tornado

The Saturday Maria and I had picked for our 50-mile bike ride seemed perfect. We set out at 7 A.M. in beautiful spring weather. The sun shone brightly. Birds sang in the trees along the roadside. At 10:30 A.M., when we stopped for a break, we both felt terrific. As we rested, though, a brisk wind sprang up. That was when our perfect day began to change.

By noon, we knew a serious thunderstorm was blowing our way. A towering bank of dark clouds had rolled up out of the southwest. A stinging wind burned our faces. There was no way to stay out of the storm. We would have to wait it out, but where?

Then things went from bad to worse. The temperature dropped suddenly. I looked up and saw that the sky now had a dark-greenish cast. Trees and crops were bent over by the wind. No animals were in sight.

Then a blue car pulled alongside our bikes. The driver ordered, "Get in!" She looked frightened, and we must have, too. We did as she said. That was when the hail started. Chunks of ice the size of golf balls pounded the windshield and dented the hood.

She sped northward with a determined look on her face. Could she outrun this storm? Maria and I looked backward at the black sky. That's when we saw it. Maria screamed. I yelled, "Tornado!" It was so close that I could see tree limbs, doors, and all sorts of other stuff that this monster had swallowed.

My heart had moved up to my throat and was beating so hard I thought it would leap from my body. I had never been so terrified. We would never outrun the tornado! The driver turned to us and said calmly, "We'll get through this. There's an overpass ahead. We'll pull in there for protection."

Once we parked, we leapt from the car and lay pressed up against the concrete wall of the overpass. Before I could count to 20, a roaring surrounded us. It sounded like a freight train passing overhead. Then, suddenly, it was over. We had made it. Some trees were uprooted. Tree branches and flowers were scattered all over. Yet everything was calm and quiet.

We got to a phone and called home. Our parents had been worried sick. But soon we were all laughing with relief. We were shaken but excited. What a story I would have to tell at school.

Whole Story Comprehension (cont.)

Directions: After you have read the story on the previous page, answer the questions below.

1. What was the author doing on the day of the tornado?

    a. bike riding

    b. playing

    c. doing homework

    d. camping

2. What was the first sign of trouble?

    a. animals disappeared

    b. crashes of thunder

    c. dark clouds and wind

    d. rain

3. As the storm got worse, what happened to the sky?

    a. It turned red.

    b. It was filled with clouds.

    c. It was gray.

    d. It had a dark-greenish cast.

4. Who rescued the kids?

    a. a woman in a blue car

    b. a farmer

    c. a friendly dog

    d. their parents

5. When did the woman and kids know they were in real danger?

    a. when they saw the hail

    b. when they saw the tornado

    c. when it started to rain hard

    d. when they got a flat tire

6. Where did the woman and the kids find shelter?

    a. under an overpass

    b. under a tree

    c. in a neighbor's house

    d. in the blue car

7. As soon as the tornado left, the kids

    a. called their parents.

    b. finished their bike ride.

    c. began to cry.

    d. went out to eat.

8. How did the kids feel when it was all over?

    a. frightened

    b. shaken but excited

    c. tired

    d. hungry

22

Enrichment

Directions: Read the information below and complete the activity.

An **exclamation** shows strong feeling. When you write an exclamation, use an exclamation mark at the end of the sentence or word.

Here is an example:

Look, there's a tornado!

Write an exclamatory sentence for each subject below. Be sure to use an exclamation mark at the end of each sentence.

1. a storm

   _____

   _____

2. something scary

   _____

   _____

3. something that surprises you

   _____

   _____

4. something that hurts you

   _____

   _____

5. a warning

   _____

   _____

Graphic Development

Directions: Tornadoes happen in many places in the United States. Tornado Alley is the area where they occur most often. Look at the map and answer "True" (T) or "False" (F).

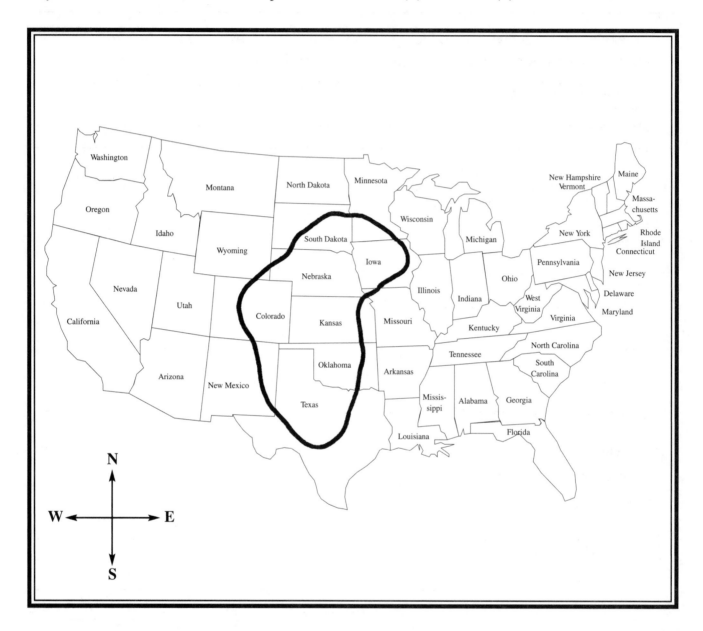

1. Most tornadoes happen in the West. _____

2. Some tornadoes happen in the East. _____

3. Many tornadoes happen in the central states. _____

4. Most of Oklahoma is in Tornado Alley. _____

5. Arizona is in Tornado Alley. _____

Sentence Comprehension

Directions: Read the following sentences carefully and answer the questions below "True" (T) or "False" (F).

> We were searching for pumpkins that we could carve into fantastic jack-o'-lanterns. We wanted to laugh at their silly faces. We wanted lots of them to decorate our front porch.

1. The kids wanted to find one big pumpkin. _____

2. The kids liked to carve pumpkins. _____

3. They would use the pumpkins to decorate their bedrooms. _____

4. They thought jack-o'-lantern faces were scary. _____

5. They wanted to give a pumpkin to a friend. _____

Word Study

Directions: Read the definition below and answer the question.

> **jack-o'-lantern**
>
> A jack-o'-lantern first meant a man carrying a lantern.

Why do you think a carved pumpkin is called a jack-o'-lantern?

_____

_____

_____

_____

Paragraph Comprehension

Directions: Read the paragraph below and answer the following questions.

So we piled into the car and drove out of town. The vegetable stand Dad remembered wasn't there! And we didn't see any others, either. Dad said that he couldn't figure out where the farmers were selling their vegetables these days. By that time, you can imagine how Tim and I felt. Maybe we wouldn't have any jack-o'-lanterns this year.

1. What did Dad take the children to find?

    a. a vegetable stand

    b. a field of pumpkins

    c. a jack-o'-lantern store

    d. a farm

2. The _____ was not there.

    a. farmer

    b. vegetable stand

    c. store

    d. field

3. Who is with the kids at the vegetable stand?

    a. no one

    b. their mom

    c. their brother

    d. their dad

4. How do you think the children felt when they couldn't find any?

    a. happy

    b. excited

    c. afraid

    d. disappointed

5. What did the children fear?

    a. They wouldn't be able to have any jack-o'-lanterns.

    b. They would get lost.

    c. They wouldn't have enough money to buy a pumpkin.

    d. They wouldn't have vegetables for dinner.

Whole Story Comprehension

Directions: Read the story below and answer the questions on the following page.

The Great Pumpkin Hunt

It was just pumpkins we were looking for that October Saturday. We were searching for pumpkins that we could carve into fantastic jack-o'-lanterns. We wanted to laugh at their silly faces. We wanted lots of them to decorate our front porch.

My brother Tim and I went to the store, where we usually get pumpkins every year. They said they only had some baby ones that were too small to carve.

Now what would we do? We went home, wondering if Mom or Dad would have any ideas. Dad said he would take us for a ride to see if a roadside vegetable stand had some pumpkins. "I can't believe they won't," he said. "It is October, after all."

So we piled into the car and drove out of town. The vegetable stand Dad remembered wasn't there! And we didn't see any others, either. Dad said that he couldn't figure out where the farmers were selling their vegetables these days. By that time, you can imagine how Tim and I felt. Maybe we wouldn't have any jack-o'-lanterns this year.

I guess Mom knew the minute she saw us that we had been unsuccessful. But she said we should all just come with her. This time she drove. Where was she taking us? A secret pumpkin store? She seemed to know exactly where she was going.

As she turned the car into the parking lot of City Hall, we saw a Farmers' Market. Wow! This is where all the farmers brought their vegetables! There were thousands of pumpkins. Huge ones, tiny ones, medium-sized ones. We'd never seen so many pumpkins to choose from!

We used some of our own money on the biggest one we'd ever had. We got some ordinary-sized ones, too. Even Dad and Mom helped carve them. We had a blast. And our porch is now a fantastic sight!

Whole Story Comprehension (cont.)

Directions: After you have read the story on the previous page, answer the questions below.

1. What day of the week did the children search for pumpkins?

    a. Monday

    b. Sunday

    c. Saturday

    d. Friday

2. Where did they first look for a pumpkin?

    a. the vegetable stand

    b. the store

    c. the Farmers' Market

    d. at a farm

3. What time of year was it?

    a. fall

    b. spring

    c. winter

    d. summer

4. Who helped them look for a vegetable stand?

    a. their dad

    b. their neighbor

    c. their mom

    d. their friend

5. Where did they find the Farmers' Market?

    a. on the roadside

    b. on a farm

    c. at City Hall

    d. outside a store

6. What did they find at the Farmers' Market?

    a. thousands of pumpkins

    b. pumpkins in all sizes

    c. farmers

    d. all of the above

7. How did they buy the biggest pumpkin?

    a. Their parents bought it for them.

    b. They used some of their own money.

    c. A farmer gave it to them.

    d. They found some money to buy it.

8. Who did the pumpkin carving?

    a. Dad

    b. Mom

    c. Tim

    d. all of them

Enrichment

Directions: Read the information in the box below to complete the activity. Read each sentence. Below it, write the feeling that is being expressed.

Exclamations

Exclamations can be used to express many feelings—fear, disappointment, excitement, amazement, and anger.

---

1. The vegetable stand Dad remembered wasn't there!

   _____

2. Wow!

   _____

3. This is where all the farmers brought their vegetables!

   _____

4. We'd never seen so many pumpkins to choose from!

   _____

5. And our porch is now a fantastic sight!

   _____

Graphic Development

Directions: Pumpkins grow on vines. They are the fruit of this kind of plant. Label each part of the pumpkin plant.

roots

stem

leaf

blossom

fruit

1.

2.

3.

4.

5.

Sentence Comprehension

Directions: Read the following sentences carefully and answer the questions below "True" (T) or "False" (F).

A young boy learns from a medicine man. He learns that plants can be used to heal.

---

1. The medicine man can teach the boy. _____

2. The medicine man uses plants. _____

3. The boy is afraid of the medicine man. _____

4. Plants can be helpful. _____

5. The boy learns about growing crops. _____

Word Study

Directions: Read the definition. Then underline the word in the sentence that means the same as *medicine man.*

---

medicine man

a kind of priest who heals sick people

The shaman used plants to heal the sick people in his tribe.

Paragraph Comprehension

Directions: Read the paragraph below and answer the following questions.

Cherry is the author and illustrator of *The Great Kapok Tree.* It was written in 1990. It teaches kids the wonders of the rain forest. Plotkin wrote *Tales of a Shaman's Apprentice,* which teaches adults about these wonders.

1. Who wrote *The Great Kapok Tree?*

   a. Cherry

   b. Plotkin

   c. a shaman

   d. a boy

2. An author writes a book. Who draws the pictures?

   a. an editor

   b. an illustrator

   c. an apprentice

   d. a publisher

3. What are "wonders" of the rain forest?

   a. mysterious things

   b. interesting things

   c. unusual things

   d. all of the above

4. *Tales of a Shaman's Apprentice* was written for

   a. children.

   b. boys.

   c. adults.

   d. scientists.

5. Which book was written for children?

   a. *The Great Kapok Tree*

   b. *Tales of a Shaman's Apprentice*

   c. both of them

   d. neither of them

Whole Story Comprehension

Directions: Read the story below and answer the questions on the following page.

Lessons of the Rain Forest

A young boy learns from a medicine man. He learns that plants can be used to heal. This tale is told in *The Shaman's Apprentice*, a book by Lynne Cherry and Mark J. Plotkin.

Cherry is the author and illustrator of *The Great Kapok Tree.* It was written in 1990. It teaches kids the wonders of the rain forest. Plotkin wrote *Tales of a Shaman's Apprentice,* which teaches adults about these wonders.

Three years ago, the two authors teamed up. They traveled to Suriname, in South America. They stayed in a Tirio Indian village. The shaman, or medicine man, showed the authors how he makes medicines from plants. "We can learn a lot from native people," says Cherry. "That's why it's important to take care of the rain forests."

Look at the drawings in *The Shaman's Apprentice,* and you'll learn a lot. "Every plant and every animal is right where it belongs," says Cherry.

Whole Story Comprehension (cont.)

Directions: After you have read the story on the previous page, answer the questions below.

1. What did Cherry and Plotkin do together?

    a. They wrote a book.

    b. They went to South America.

    c. The grew plants.

    d. both a and b

2. What does a shaman do?

    a. He is a farmer.

    b. He heals sick people.

    c. He writes books.

    d. He leads his tribe.

3. What did the shaman show the authors?

    a. how to heal people

    b. pictures of the rain forest

    c. how to make medicines

    d. the sites of South America

4. In the book, who teaches the boy?

    a. the rain forest animals

    b. the medicine man

    c. Mark Plotkin

    d. his parents

5. Why did Plotkin write *Tales of a Shaman's Apprentice?*

    a. to teach people about the Tirio Indians

    b. to teach people about South America

    c. to teach children about the rain forest

    d. to teach adults about the rain forest

6. What does Cherry say about the book's drawings?

    a. They are pretty.

    b. They are interesting.

    c. They can teach us things about the rain forest.

    d. They are colorful.

7. *Tales of a Shaman's Apprentice* is probably

    a. fiction.

    b. nonfiction.

    c. both fiction and nonfiction.

8. In our culture, a shaman would be called

    a. a teacher.

    b. a doctor.

    c. the president.

    d. a policeman.

Enrichment

Directions: Read the information below and complete the activity.

A **synonym** is a word that means the same or almost the same as another word.

The word *apprentice* is a synonym for the word *student*.

A **student** *learns how to do something from an expert.*

An **apprentice** *learns how to do something from an expert.*

Write a synonym for each word below.

1. shaman

   _____

2. author

   _____

3. artist

   _____

4. student

   _____

5. village

   _____

Graphic Development

Directions: Use the map to answer the questions "True" (T) or "False" (F).

1. Suriname is the largest country in South America. _____

2. Guyana is west of Suriname. _____

3. Part of Suriname touches the Atlantic Ocean. _____

4. Suriname is near the Pacific Ocean. _____

5. Brazil is south of Suriname. _____

Sentence Comprehension

Directions: Read the following sentences carefully and answer the questions below "True" (T) or "False" (F).

It's a giant squid. No one has ever seen a giant squid alive. Scientists have been able to study only a few body parts.

1. People can see giant squid in the ocean. _____

2. Scientists are interested in giant squid. _____

3. Giant squid are mysterious. _____

4. Parts of giant squid are all that scientists have seen. _____

5. The only giant squid people have seen are dead. _____

Word Study

Directions: The story on the next page is about a giant squid called Squidzilla. Read the information below and then write about how this squid might have gotten its name.

Godzilla

Godzilla is a monster from the movies. This monster looked very much like a dinosaur. He was about 124 feet tall and weighed about 22,000 pounds.

If a giant squid is named Squidzilla, what does that tell you about it?

_____

_____

_____

_____

_____

Paragraph Comprehension

Directions: Read the paragraph below and answer the following questions.

Squidzilla is the most complete giant squid ever studied. It has all eight of its arms and two tentacles! The squid is in great shape. When the dead squid landed in a fisherman's net, he froze it so it wouldn't rot. Then it was flown to New York City.

1. Who found the giant squid?

    a. a fisherman

    b. scientists

    c. a swimmer

    d. a museum owner

2. How is Squidzilla different from other giant squid studied?

    a. It is the biggest one.

    b. It has a name.

    c. It is the most complete.

    d. It didn't rot.

3. What would have happened to the squid if the fisherman hadn't frozen it?

    a. It would have lived.

    b. It would have killed someone.

    c. It would have rotted.

    d. It would have swam away.

4. How was the squid caught?

    a. The fisherman caught and killed it.

    b. The fisherman found it dead in his net.

    c. It was hunted by squid hunters.

    d. It was caught in a trap.

5. How did the squid get to New York City?

    a. by boat

    b. by truck

    c. by train

    d. by plane

Whole Story Comprehension

Directions: Read the story below and answer the questions on the following page.

Secrets of the Giant Squid

It lies still and wet in a giant metal tank wrapped with chains. The case is too big to fit through any of the doors in New York City's American Museum of Natural History. On the case, are the letters S-Q-U-I-D-Z-I-L-L-A.

"We keep it chained up so it doesn't get out," jokes Neil Landman. He's a scientist at the museum. There is no way the creature could get out—it's dead. But what exactly is it?

It's a giant squid. No one has ever seen a giant squid alive. Scientists have been able to study only a few body parts. This month, museum visitors can get a look at the monster. Squidzilla will be displayed in a huge plastic case.

Squidzilla is the most complete giant squid ever studied. It has all eight of its arms and two tentacles! The squid is in great shape. When the dead squid landed in a fisherman's net, he froze it so it wouldn't rot. Then it was flown to New York City.

Squidzilla is 25 feet long and weighs 200 pounds. At first, the scientists thought they had a baby giant squid. Its arms are much shorter than others they had seen. Scientists think giant squid can be as much as 60 feet long and weigh more than a ton.

After studying it, the scientists decided it is a full-grown male. They think females have longer arms. Giant squid swim in deep waters. Scientists aren't sure how many giant squid there are. They don't even know where they live. Don't hold your breath waiting for answers. As long as they stay deep in the ocean's dark waters, giant squid will probably remain a mystery.

Whole Story Comprehension (cont.)

Directions: After you have read the story on the previous page, answer the questions below.

1. What is Squidzilla?

   a. the biggest squid in the ocean

   b. a monster

   c. a dead giant squid

   d. a baby giant squid

2. Why couldn't the squid get out of the tank?

   a. It is chained in.

   b. The tank is locked.

   c. It would have nowhere to go.

   d. It is dead.

3. At first scientists thought the squid was

   a. the biggest they had ever seen.

   b. a baby squid.

   c. pregnant.

   d. alive.

4. Scientists think Squidzilla's arms are short because

   a. it's a boy.

   b. part of the arms broke off.

   c. it's a girl.

   d. it's a baby.

5. Scientists don't know much about giant squid because

   a. they are dangerous.

   b. they are fast swimmers.

   c. they live in deep, dark waters.

   d. they hide from scientists.

6. Where do giant squid live?

   a. in dark caves

   b. in shallow ocean areas

   c. in the Atlantic Ocean

   d. no one really knows

7. Squidzilla weighs about as much as

   a. a bus.

   b. a house.

   c. a large man.

   d. a big dog.

8. Where can people see Squidzilla?

   a. in the ocean

   b. at Sea World

   c. in a museum

   d. in a big metal ball

Enrichment

Directions: Read the information below and complete the activity.

When numbers are used in writing, use the written word for the number unless it is the number 10 or larger.

Here are some examples:

I have **two** dogs.

My sister is **16** years old.

Read each sentence below. Write the correct form of the number on the line.

1. The squid weighs _____ pounds.
   (two hundred)

2. The fisherman found _____ squid.
   (one)

3. Squidzilla is _____ feet long.
   (twenty-five)

4. The squid has _____ arms.
   (eight)

5. It has _____ tentacles.
   (two)

6. Some giant squid can be _____ feet long.
   (sixty)

Graphic Development

Directions: Read the definitions for the body parts of a squid. Then label the drawing.

Squid Body Parts

head: has a brain

eyes: eyes can be 10 inches around

fins: has very small fins at the back of its body

mantle: the main body

arms: has eight arms with suckers on them

tentacles: longer than the arms and used for feeding

funnel: a tube for breathing, squirting ink, and laying eggs

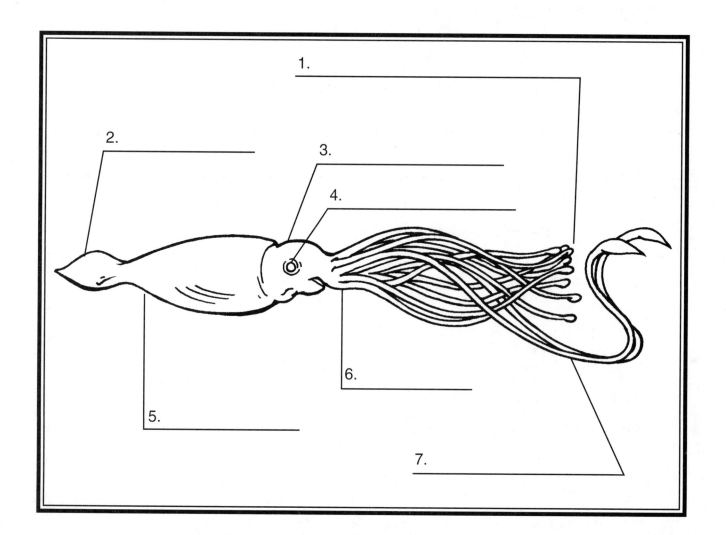

Sentence Comprehension

Directions: Read the following sentences carefully and answer the questions below "True" (T) or "False" (F).

> Our nearest star (the sun) is hard to understand. It is a loudly exploding ball of fiery gas.

1. The sun is our nearest star. _____

2. Scientists know a lot about the sun. _____

3. The sun is a small ball of light. _____

4. The sun is made of fiery gas. _____

5. There is a lot to learn about the sun. _____

Word Study

Directions: Read the definition below. Then answer "True" (T) or "False" (F) for each sentence.

> **telescope**
>
> a tool used to look at far away objects

1. The sun can be seen with a telescope. _____

2. A telescope can be used to see inside your body. _____

3. You can look at small insects with a telescope. _____

4. You can see a far away planet with a telescope. _____

5. A telescope makes far away objects seem closer. _____

Paragraph Comprehension

Directions: Read the paragraph below and answer the following questions.

Scientists hope to predict solar weather. They will learn its effects on Earth. "We used to think the inside of the sun was fairly simple," says Arizona astronomer John Harvey. "But that was before we had the capability to see into it."

1. What do scientists hope to do someday?

    a. They hope to see the sun.

    b. They want to travel to the sun.

    c. They want to predict the weather on the sun.

    d. They hope to see the Earth with a telescope.

2. What did scientists think about the inside of the sun?

    a. It was hard to understand.

    b. It was easy to understand.

    c. It was cold inside.

    d. It was too far away to see.

3. An astronomer

    a. can study the sun.

    b. can travel through space.

    c. can make a telescope.

    d. is a weatherman.

4. The sun's weather

    a. is always nice.

    b. has rain and snow.

    c. affects the earth.

    d. is always stormy.

5. Scientists can

    a. see inside the sun.

    b. only see the outside of the sun.

    c. change the sun's weather.

    d. none of the above

Whole Story Comprehension

Directions: Read the story below and answer the questions on the following page.

Great Ball of Fire!

The sun seems to be a quiet ball of light and heat. It tans sunbathers and helps plants grow. But our nearest star is hard to understand. It is a loudly exploding ball of fiery gas. Sometimes it whips up big storms on its surface.

This stormy weather can cause problems on Earth. Solar storms can make compass needles point the wrong way. They can even knock out electric and phone service.

Now scientists are using tools on Earth to "look inside" the sun. A weatherman can predict rain and snow. Someday they may be able to forecast solar storms.

SOHO is a spacecraft packed with telescopes. It circles the sun taking pictures.

Scientists were surprised by what they found. SOHO found rivers and winds of super hot gas beneath the surface of the sun.

Scientists will learn even more of the sun's secrets. On August 25, 1997, NASA launched another craft that tracks the solar wind. These are fiery particles of the sun that fly through the solar system. They affect weather on the planets.

Scientists hope to predict solar weather. They will learn its effects on Earth. "We used to think the inside of the sun was fairly simple," says Arizona astronomer John Harvey. "But that was before we had the capability to see into it."

Whole Story Comprehension (cont.)

Directions: After you have read the story on the previous page, answer the questions below.

1. Does the sun have loud explosions?

    a. yes

    b. no

    c. no one really knows

    d. only in the summer

2. What troubles can the sun cause on Earth?

    a. It can make compass needles point the wrong way.

    b. It can affect electric power.

    c. It can affect phone service.

    d. all of the above

3. What do astronomers want to predict?

    a. rain and snow

    b. the Earth's weather

    c. solar storms

    d. the size of the sun

4. Solar wind is

    a. like a windy day on Earth.

    b. fiery particles of the sun.

    c. strong wind on Earth caused by the sun.

    d. inside the sun.

5. What spacecraft circles the sun?

    a. NASA

    b. a telescope

    c. SOHO

    d. the solar craft

6. *Predict* means to

    a. guess.

    b. study.

    c. learn about.

    d. see.

7. Which word means the same or almost the same as *predict*?

    a. storm

    b. forecast

    c. effect

    d. solar

8. A solar storm is a storm on/in

    a. the sun.

    b. the earth.

    c. another planet.

    d. the solar system.

Enrichment

Directions: Read the information below and complete the activity.

Many words have more than one definition, or meaning.

How the word is used in a sentence determines what that meaning is.

---

1. A car needs *gas* in order to move.

   Explain this definition of gas.

   _____

   _____

   _____

2. The sun is a fiery ball of *gas*.

   Explain this definition of gas.

   _____

   _____

   _____

Graphic Development

Directions: Read the information below and answer the questions.

SOHO stands for Solar and Heliospheric Observatory. SOHO has two sections. The top section holds all of the scientific tools. The bottom section holds tools for control, power, and talking to Earth.

This is what SOHO looks like:

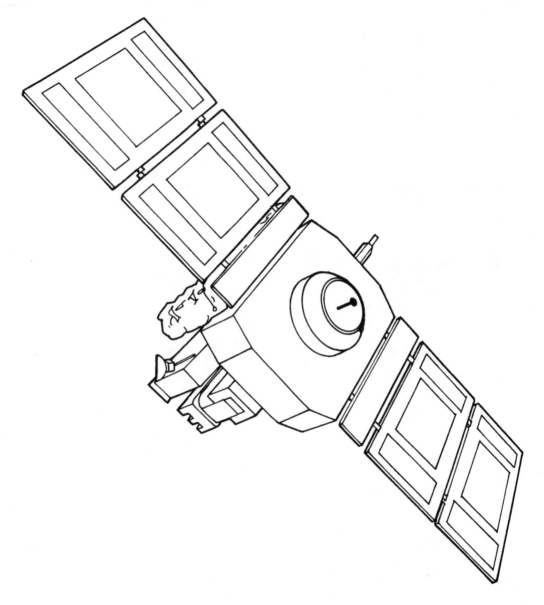

1. Would a telescope be in the top of SOHO?_____

2. Which part of SOHO would take pictures of the sun? _____

3. Which part of SOHO would communicate with Earth? _____

Sentence Comprehension

Directions: Read the following sentences carefully and answer the questions below "True" (T) or "False" (F).

The eggs belonged to titanosaurs (tie-tan-o-sores). These dinosaurs had long necks. They ate plants.

---

1. Titanosaurs are dinosaurs. _____

2. They are meat eaters. _____

3. Titanosaurs hatched from eggs. _____

4. These dinosaurs had long necks. _____

5. They are reptiles. _____

Word Study

Directions: Read the definition and answer the questions.

---

dinosaur

terrible lizard or marvelous lizard

---

1. What kind of animal was a dinosaur (bird, mammal, reptile)?

   _____

2. Why do you think they are called terrible and marvelous?

   _____

   _____

   _____

Paragraph Comprehension

Directions: Read the paragraph below and answer the following questions.

Millions of years ago, a group of dinosaurs walked along a riverbank in South America. They had chosen the place to lay their eggs. One by one, the babies started to hatch.

---

1. From this paragraph, we can tell that dinosaurs

   a. sometimes traveled in groups.

   b. always laid eggs beside the river.

   c. were mean.

   d. ate meat.

2. Where did they choose to lay their eggs?

   a. in the ocean

   b. in a river

   c. beside a river

   d. in a field

3. How are baby dinosaurs born?

   a. They hatch from eggs.

   b. They are born alive.

   c. They grow inside of a pouch.

   d. They develop in the water.

4. How long ago did these dinosaurs lay the eggs?

   a. a few years ago

   b. about ten years ago

   c. a hundred years ago

   d. many, many years ago

5. The baby dinosaurs were born

   a two at a time.

   b three at a time.

   c all at once.

   d one at a time.

50

Whole Story Comprehension

Directions: Read the story below and answer the questions on the following page.

Dino Eggs by the Dozen

Millions of years ago, a group of dinosaurs walked along a riverbank in South America. They had chosen the place to lay their eggs. One by one, the babies started to hatch.

Then there was a big flood. The dinosaur nursery was lost forever.

Well, not quite forever. In 1998, a group of scientists found the eggs. They found them in a dry area in Argentina.

They saw a field covered with rocks. The rocks were the size of grapefruits. They took a closer look. The "rocks" were really dinosaur eggs. "There were thousands of eggs all over the place," says Luis Chiappe, one of the team's leaders.

The eggs belonged to titanosaurs (tie-tan-o-sores). These dinosaurs had long necks. They ate plants.

An adult titanosaur was more than 50 feet long. Babies were about 15 inches long. That's the size of a small dog.

The flood buried the eggs in mud. The mud helped preserve the babies inside. One egg contained 32 tiny teeth. Others held patches of scaly skin.

The scientists returned to learn more about the dinosaurs. They hoped to answer more questions. With so many eggs to study, those answers may be just waiting to hatch.

Whole Story Comprehension *(cont.)*

Directions: After you have read the story on the previous page, answer the questions below.

1. Who found the dinosaur eggs?

   a. a group of children

   b. animals

   c. scientists

   d. astronauts

2. Why did the eggs look like rocks?

   a. They had turned into fossils.

   b. They looked like pebbles.

   c. They were buried under the ground.

   d. They were round.

3. What is a flood?

   a. a long time with no water

   b. a big snow storm

   c. water that covers the land

   d like a tornado

4. Why was the nursery "lost forever"?

   a. The eggs never hatched.

   b. The older dinosaurs left.

   c. The eggs washed into the ocean.

   d. The dinosaurs destroyed them.

5. Baby titanosaurs were

   a. about the length of a pencil.

   b. about the length of a car.

   c. about the length of a computer keyboard.

   d. about the length of your thumb.

6. What preserved the eggs in the flood?

   a. the mothers

   b. mud

   c. the water

   d. a nest

7. What was found inside the eggs?

   a. live dinosaur babies

   b. mud

   c. teeth and skin

   d. skeletons

8. Why did the scientists return to Argentina?

   a. They wanted to find fossils of other dinosaurs.

   b. They wanted to live there.

   c. They wanted to study more eggs.

   d. They wanted to find a live titanosaur.

Enrichment

Directions: Read the information and complete the activity.

Read the following sentence:

The rocks (eggs) were the size of grapefruits.

The author compared the eggs to something familiar. This helps us to "picture" the size of the eggs.

Complete the sentences below using comparisons. The first one has been done for you.

1. The cookie was as big as a *pancake*.

2. The bird was as small as _____.

3. The tree was the size of _____.

4. The music was as loud as _____.

5. The wind sounded like _____.

Graphic Development

Directions: Complete the web using information from the story.

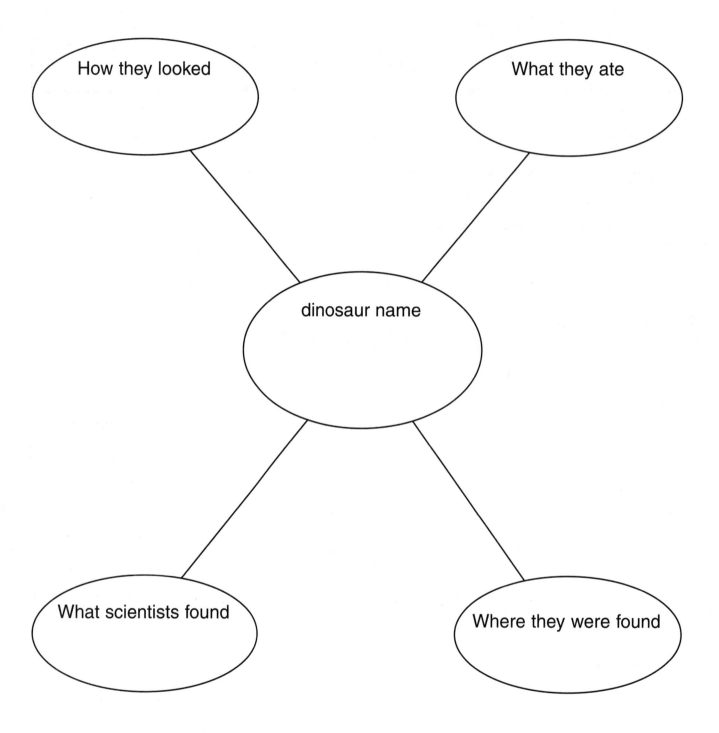

Sentence Comprehension

Directions: Read the following sentences carefully and answer the questions below "True" (T) or "False" (F).

> The *Endurance* was just 100 miles from Antarctica when ice suddenly closed around it. It would be months before the ice melted and the ship could sail.

1. The *Endurance* was an airplane. _____

2. It was traveling to Antarctica. _____

3. The ship had a problem on the trip. _____

4. Ice helped the ship travel in the water. _____

5. The ship had trouble sailing to Antarctica. _____

Word Study

Directions: Read the definition below and answer the question.

> **endurance**
>
> the ability to handle hard times or problems

The ship's name was *Endurance*. What does this name tell you about the ship?

_____

_____

_____

_____

Paragraph Comprehension

Directions: Read the paragraph below and answer the following questions.

> After 10 months, the ice began to crush the ship. Shackleton ordered the men to leave the ship. The sailors were stranded on an island. So Shackleton set out to sea with five strong men. He left the others behind. They sailed and rowed 800 miles in a tiny boat.

1. Why did Shackleton order the men to leave the ship?

    a. so they could travel around the world

    b. to continue their trip

    c. the ship was unsafe

    d. to find more sled dogs

2. They left the ship after how long?

    a. more than a year

    b. almost a year

    c. half a year

    d. a few weeks

3. What problem did they have?

    a. Ice crushed the ship.

    b. They ran out of food.

    c. The men were too cold to travel.

    d. The ship began to sink.

4. Why did Shackleton leave the men on the island?

    a. He went to get help.

    b. He only wanted to save himself.

    c. He was afraid of the men.

    d. He thought they would all die.

5. How did they go get help?

    a. They flew in an airplane.

    b. They used a tiny boat.

    c. They used the crushed ship.

    d. They traveled with sled dogs.

Whole Story Comprehension

Directions: Read the story below and answer the questions on the following page.

Antarctic Shipwreck!

When Ernest Shackleton packed for his trip in 1914, he seemed ready for anything. He and his 27-man crew filled their ship with food, tents, warm clothes, and sled dogs. The ship was called the *Endurance*. They hoped to be the first people to travel across Antarctica.

But the men did not make it. Instead, they made history in a story of survival.

The *Endurance* was just 100 miles from Antarctica when ice suddenly closed around it. It would be months before the ice melted and the ship could sail.

The ship drifted with the ice. The sailors tried to keep warm. They passed the time by playing cards. They built "dogloos" for their sled dogs.

After 10 months, the ice began to crush the ship. Shackleton ordered the men to leave the ship. The sailors were stranded on an island. So Shackleton set out to sea with five strong men. He left the others behind. They sailed and rowed 800 miles in a tiny boat.

Four months later, Shackleton returned to rescue his crew. They laughed and hugged. All 28 men of the *Endurance* trip survived. How? Perhaps because Shackleton was a true hero. As the explorer said, "If you're a leader, you've got to keep going."

Whole Story Comprehension (cont.)

Directions: After you have read the story on the previous page, answer the questions below.

1. What did the men pack for their trip?

    a. warm clothes

    b. tents

    c. food

    d. all of the above

2. *Survival* means

    a. to go on a trip.

    b. to sail in a ship.

    c. to stay alive.

    d. to row a boat.

3. The *Endurance* was traveling to

    a. Antarctica.

    b. Africa.

    c. Australia.

    d. Argentina.

4. What stopped the ship from moving?

    a. the cold weather

    b. the wind

    c. ice

    d. an island

5. What is a "dogloo"?

    a. a dog treat

    b. a winter house for a dog

    c. a kind of sled

    d. a sweater for a dog

6. Where was the crew stranded?

    a. on Antarctica

    b. on an island

    c. in the ship

    d. on a small boat

7. How many men rowed the tiny boat 800 miles?

    a. three

    b. six

    c. five

    d. eight

8. How many of the crew members died?

    a. only one

    b. five

    c. ten

    d. none of them

Enrichment

Directions: Read the information below and complete the activity.

Use one of the following words to complete each sentence below.

stranded	endure	survive	drifted	rescue

1. The men kept warm so they could _____.

2. The ship _____ at sea.

3. They were _____ on an island.

4. They wondered if someone would _____ them.

5. They all had to _____ the cold weather.

Write a paragraph using all of the words in the box above.

_____

_____

_____

_____

_____

_____

_____

Graphic Development

Directions: Use the map to answer the questions "True" (T) or "False" (F).

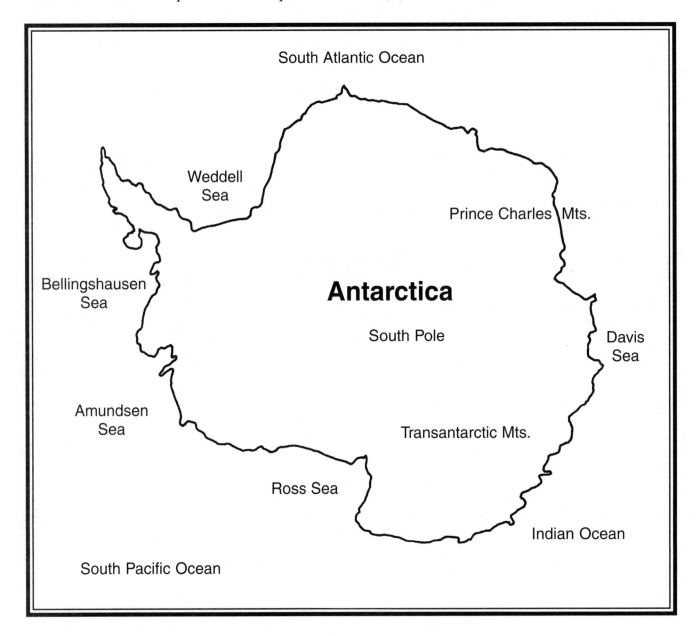

1. The South Pole is in the center of Antarctica. _____

2. Three oceans surround Antarctica. _____

3. The Weddell Sea is near the Indian Ocean. _____

4. Antarctica has mountains. _____

5. Ross Sea and Davis Sea are near the Pacific Ocean. _____

Sentence Comprehension

Directions: Read the following sentences carefully and answer the questions below "True" (T) or "False" (F).

Meyer is a scientist. He wants to understand why sharks act the way they do.

---

1. All scientists study sharks. _____

2. Meyer studies sharks. _____

3. Meyer can study how sharks act. _____

4. Scientists cannot study sharks. _____

5. Some scientists study sharks. _____

Word Study

Directions: Read the definition and explain the meaning of the following sentence.

---

extinct

no longer alive or no more left

Some kinds of sharks will be extinct within 10 years.

_____

_____

_____

_____

Paragraph Comprehension

Directions: Read the paragraph below and answer the following questions.

Humans have always been afraid of sharks, but attacks are rare. Sharks like to eat fatter animals, such as seals. In a bad year, sharks may kill 15 swimmers. This is mostly by mistake. To a shark, flapping feet may look like a seal or a fish.

---

1. Do sharks attack people?

    a. yes, all the time

    b. no, not at all

    c. yes, but not often

    d. yes, but only at night

2. Why do sharks attack people?

    a. They think they are seals or fish.

    b. They are hungry.

    c. They like to kill people.

    d. They will attack anything they see.

3. What do flapping feet look like to a shark?

    a. another shark

    b. a boat

    c. a seal or fish

    d. a person in the water

4. Why would a shark rather eat a seal than a person?

    a. They are fatter.

    b. They are smaller.

    c. They taste better.

    d. They are easier to attack.

5. How many shark attacks resulting in the loss of human life happen in a year?

    a. more than 20

    b. 15 or less

    c. between 20 and 50

    d. none

Whole Story Comprehension

Directions: Read the story below and answer the questions on the following page.

Sharks: Under Attack!

Carl Meyer is on a small motorboat near Hawaii. He tries an unusual rope trick. He is roping a shark! Meyer has caught a six-foot tiger shark with a hook. Now he pulls the shark in and ties it to the boat. The shark shows hundreds of very sharp teeth. Meyer whispers, "No biting, no biting!"

Meyer is a scientist. He wants to understand why sharks act the way they do. There is not so much to fear from sharks. We can learn a lot from them.

Humans have always been afraid of sharks, but attacks are rare. Sharks like to eat fatter animals, such as seals. In a bad year, sharks may kill 15 swimmers. This is mostly by mistake. To a shark, flapping feet may look like a seal or a fish.

But humans are a danger to sharks. Millions of sharks are killed each year. At this rate, some kinds of sharks will be extinct within 10 years.

Sharks are amazing animals. They were around before the dinosaurs! A shark's body can fight off sickness better than a human's body. "They have simple bodies," scientist John Marchalonis says, "but they do a good job."

Many people study sharks to help protect them. Governments are trying to cut down on shark hunting. In many places, there are limits on how many sharks a person can catch. California passed a law against taking white sharks from state waters.

Gilbert Van Dykhuizan says, "Sharks are here for a reason, not to attack men, women, and children."

Whole Story Comprehension *(cont.)*

Directions: After you have read the story on the previous page, answer the questions below.

1. What did Meyer say to the shark he caught?

    a. hold still

    b. don't move

    c. no biting

    d. it's okay

2. Why do many people kill sharks?

    a. They are afraid of them.

    b. They like to eat them.

    c. They want to make them extinct.

    d. They are ugly.

3. What can a shark do better than a human?

    a. digest food

    b. fight off sickness

    c. see things

    d. none of the above

4. In California, it is against the law to

    a. remove a white shark from the water.

    b. study sharks.

    c. swim with sharks.

    d. take pictures of sharks.

5. Governments are trying to

    a. cut down on shark hunting.

    b. get rid of sharks.

    c. learn more about sharks.

    d. protect people from sharks.

6. What is the greatest danger to sharks?

    a. other sharks

    b. the government

    c. people

    d. scientists

7. Why do scientists study sharks?

    a. to learn from them

    b. to protect them

    c. to get rid of them

    d. both a and b

8. Sharks have been around longer than

    a. dinosaurs.

    b. people.

    c. both a and b

    d. none of the above

Enrichment

Directions: Read the information below and then complete the activity.

An apostrophe and s are used to show that to which something belongs.

*A **shark's** body can fight off sickness better than a **human's** body.*

The sentence talks about a body that belongs to a shark and a body that belongs to a human.

Complete each sentence by writing a word with apostrophe s.

1. The _____ jacket was unzipped.

2. The _____ cry was very loud.

3. My _____ mother came to get her.

4. That _____ growl is scary.

5. My _____ dress is pretty.

Now create three more sentences using a word with apostrophe s in each sentence.

6. _____

    _____

7. _____

    _____

8. _____

    _____

Graphic Development

Directions: Use the shark diagram to answer the questions.

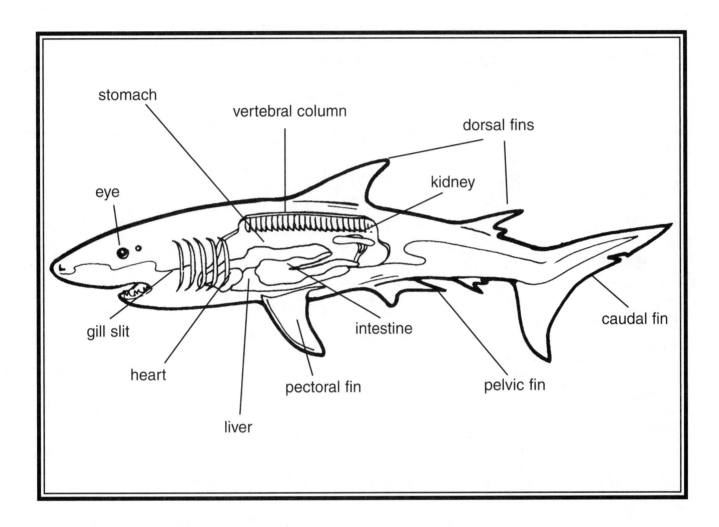

1. What is the name of a shark's tail fin? _____

2. What kind of slits are on the shark's side? _____

3. What are the fins on the top of the shark? _____

4. What is the fin in front of the caudal fin? _____

5. How many dorsal fins does a shark have? _____

Sentence Comprehension

Directions: Read the following sentences carefully and answer the questions below "True" (T) or "False" (F).

Camels are often used in this dry, sandy part of Africa. Camels can go for weeks without drinking water.

---

1. Camels need to drink water often. _____

2. Camels live in Africa. _____

3. Africa has deserts. _____

4. Parts of Africa are dry and sandy. _____

5. Camels do well in dry weather. _____

Word Study

Directions: Read the definitions. Then, write "A" or "B" to tell which definition is being used in each sentence.

---

treasure

    A. riches

    B. to hold or to value

_____ 1. The man kept his treasure in the bank.

_____ 2. The woman treasured the picture of her son.

_____ 3. He treasured his time reading books.

_____ 4. He found a buried treasure.

Paragraph Comprehension

Directions: Read the paragraph below and answer the following questions.

In 1996, there was only one librarian in Garissa. Garissa is an area of Kenya. It is in Africa. His library had 24,000 books, but not many people came to read them. "We had to find a way to reach the people. They were not coming to us."

1. From this paragraph, you can tell that
    a. books are important to the librarian.
    b. the librarian didn't have many books.
    c. there weren't enough books for the people.
    d. the librarian didn't like books.

2. Garissa is
    a. the name of the librarian.
    b. an area of Kenya.
    c. the name of the library.
    d. the name of a book.

3. What problem did the librarian have?
    a. He didn't have enough books.
    b. He had no place to put his books.
    c. People didn't come to read his books.
    d. He was the only librarian.

4. Why do you think the people didn't come to read the books?
    a. They didn't know how to read.
    b. They lived too far away.
    c. They didn't like to read.
    d. They didn't like the books at the library.

5. What did the librarian want to do?
    a. bring the books to the people
    b. teach people to read
    c. get more books
    d. a and c

Whole Story Comprehension

Directions: Read the story below and answer the questions on the following page.

Special Delivery

In 1996, there was only one librarian in Garissa. Garissa is an area of Kenya. It is in Africa. His library had 24,000 books, but not many people came to read them. "We had to find a way to reach the people. They were not coming to us."

Then, he had an idea. He would take the library to the people. He knew just what to do for desert travel. The Mobile Camel Library was born!

Camels are often used in this dry, sandy part of Africa. Camels can go for weeks without drinking water. Their hooves are flat and wide. This is perfect for desert travel. They don't sink in the sand. Also, a camel can carry very heavy loads.

Now three camels travel twice a month. They carry boxes filled with books. Kids are happy when the library visits. In the village of Bulla Iftin, one boy said he treasures his time with each book. "I really want the book to stay in my head," he says.

What happens if someone loses a book? Library fines are pretty stiff. "If a community loses books," the librarian says, "we do not go back."

Whole Story Comprehension *(cont.)*

Directions: After you have read the story on the previous page, answer the questions below.

1. What did the librarian decide to do?

    a. buy more books

    b. bring the books to the people

    c. raise camels instead

    d. become an author

2. What did the librarian use to carry the books?

    a. a backpack

    b. camels

    c. a library assistant

    d. a truck

3. Why are camels' feet good for traveling in sand?

    a. They have thick hooves.

    b. They don't get hot.

    c. They are wide and flat.

    d. They can run fast.

4. Camels can

    a. move very quickly.

    b. see in the dark.

    c. carry heavy loads.

    d. a and c

5. Why do you think the children are happy when the library visits?

    a. They have never seen camels.

    b. They like to read books.

    c. They get to miss school.

    d. all of the above

6. How often does the library come to visit?

    a. once a month

    b. two times a month

    c. every six months

    d. twice a week

7. What happens if a book is lost?

    a. The library won't return.

    b. They have to pay a fine.

    c. They have to buy a new book.

    d. The librarian gets mad.

8. Why did the librarian want to take books to people?

    a. so they could learn new things

    b. so they could enjoy books

    c. so they could become better readers

    d. all of the above

Enrichment

Directions: Read the information below and complete the activity.

Quotation marks show what someone is saying.

Read the following example:

"I really want the book to stay in my head," he says.

Read the sentences below. Write quotation marks around what is being said.

1. What time do we need to leave? asked Kelly.

2. Gina said, We really need to invite Jimmy.

3. Do you think he'll want to go? asked Mike.

4. I think he will, said Leah.

5. They all said, Okay, let's give him a call.

Now create three more sentences using quotations marks.

6. _____

   _____

7. _____

   _____

8. _____

   _____

Graphic Development

Directions: Use the map to answer the questions.

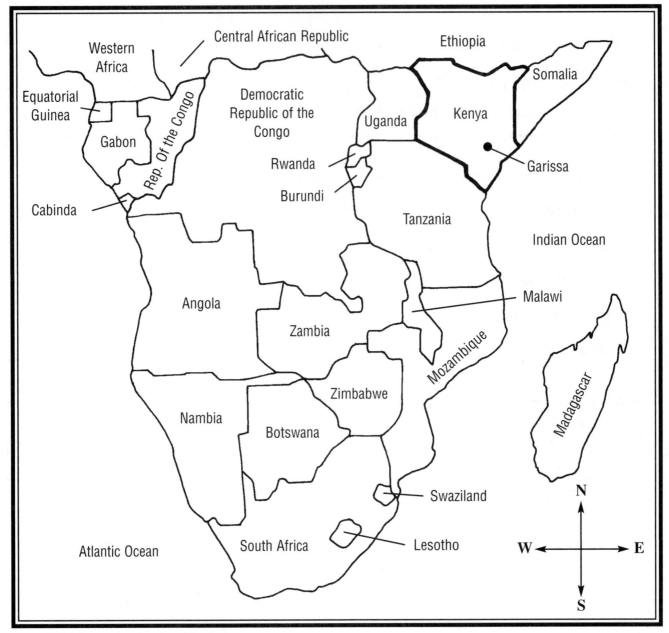

1. Which ocean touches Kenya? _____

2. Is Garissa in east or west Kenya? _____

3. What country is north of Kenya? _____

4. What country is closest to Garissa? _____

5. The Atlantic Ocean touches which side of Africa? _____

Sentence Comprehension

Directions: Read the following sentences carefully and answer the questions "True" (T) or "False" (F).

Who's afraid of the big, black bat? People who don't know how helpful bats can be.

1. Bats are helpful. _____

2. Bats always hurt people. _____

3. Some people are afraid of bats. _____

4. Many people don't understand bats. _____

Word Study

Directions: Read the definitions and then complete the activity.

conservation

protection of something

international

involving more than one country

There is a group called Bat Conservation International. Explain what you think this group does and why.

_____

_____

_____

_____

_____

Paragraph Comprehension

Directions: Read the paragraph below and answer the following questions.

Bats, not people, should be afraid. Today, 20 kinds of bats are endangered. Some people burn them out of caves or bury them inside their homes.

---

1. Who should be more afraid?

   a. bats

   b. farmers

   c. people

   d. other animals

2. Why should bats be afraid?

   a. People try to kill them.

   b. They fly in the dark.

   c. There isn't enough food for them.

   d. They can get lost.

3. How many kinds of bats are endangered?

   a. 10

   b. more than 100

   c. 20

   d. 15

4. What do some people do to bats?

   a. They keep them as pets.

   b. They throw rocks at them.

   c. They burn them out of their caves.

   d. They catch them in nets.

5. *Endangered* means

   a. disappearing.

   b. hurt.

   c. smart.

   d. unhappy.

Whole Story Comprehension

Directions: Read the story below and answer the questions on the following page.

A Spooky Friend

Who's afraid of the big, black bat? People who don't know how helpful bats can be.

Bats help farmers. They eat bugs that hurt crops. There is a group of Mexican free-tailed bats in Texas. They gobble up 250 tons of insects every night! Bats also snack on flies and mosquitoes.

Bats are also helpful to cacti. They move pollen from cactus to cactus. They spread the seeds around, too. Birds and other desert animals depend on cactus plants for food.

Bats, not people, should be afraid. Today, 20 kinds of bats are endangered. Some people burn them out of caves or bury them inside their homes.

The good news is that some people are trying to protect bats. There is a group called Bat Conservation International. It has built more than 100 gates to cover the fronts of caves and mine shafts. These gates let bats in but keep people out.

Many bats live in Austin, Texas. One million bats fly out from under the Congress Avenue Bridge at sunset. The people like them. This is the largest bat colony in any city in the world.

So don't be afraid if you see a bat. The scariest things about them are the tales people tell.

Whole Story Comprehension *(cont.)*

Directions: After you have read the story on the previous page, answer the questions below.

1. When bats eat bugs, they

    a. help crops.

    b. hurt people.

    c. make a mess.

    d. fly in the day.

2. Bats also eat

    a. meat.

    b. birds.

    c. flies.

    d. grass.

3. How do bats help cacti?

    a. They eat them.

    b. They eat their flowers.

    c. They spread pollen.

    d. They live in them.

4. Gates are put on caves to

    a. keep people out.

    b. keep bats in.

    c. protect people.

    d. get rid of bats.

5. In Texas, some bats live

    a. in houses.

    b. under a bridge.

    c. under water.

    d. out in the open.

6. A *colony* is a

    a. group.

    b. house.

    c. cave.

    d. kind of bat.

7. The scariest thing about bats is

    a. their wings.

    b. their feet.

    c. their faces.

    d. stories people tell.

8. People should

    a. not be afraid of bats.

    b. help protect bats.

    c. learn more about bats.

    d. all of the above

Enrichment

Directions: Read the information below and then complete the activity.

A *contraction* is two words put together. Some of the letters are left out and an apostrophe is put in their place.

Here are some examples:

I've = I have

you're = you are

Write the two words that make up each contraction.

1. wouldn't _____ _____

2. he's _____ _____

3. who's _____ _____

4. we're _____ _____

5. you've _____ _____

6. she'll _____ _____

Graphic Development

Directions: Look at the diagram in the box below. Use the information to write about the body of a bat.

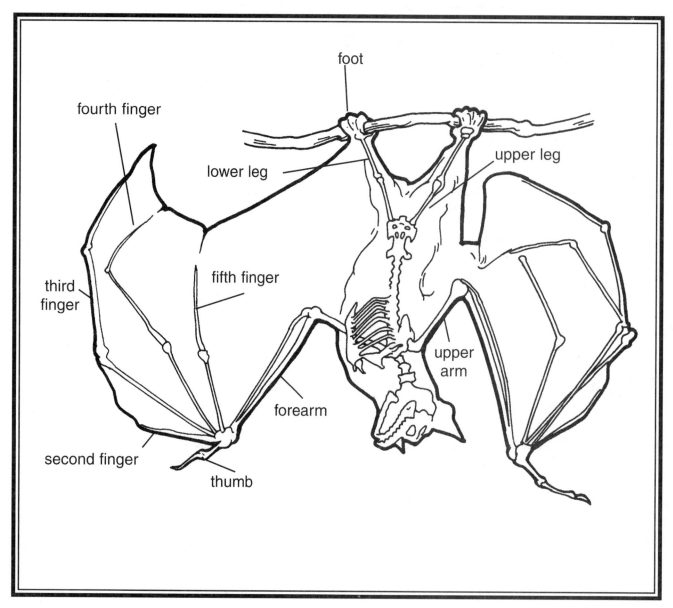

_____

_____

_____

_____

_____

Sentence Comprehension

Directions: Read the following sentence carefully and answer the questions below "True" (T) or "False" (F).

Scientists think *Prospector* may find ice on the moon.

---

1. Scientists know that there is ice on the moon. _____

2. *Prospector* is going to the moon. _____

3. Scientists are interested in the moon. _____

4. *Prospector* can teach us about the moon. _____

5. It is impossible to study the moon. _____

Word Study

Directions: Read the definition. Then rewrite each sentence using your own words. The first one has been done for you.

---

lunar

relating to the moon

---

1. The spacecraft is called the *Lunar Prospector*.

   Prospector is a spacecraft that goes to the moon. _____

2. The astronauts made a lunar landing.

   _____

3. The Apollo missions were lunar space trips.

   _____

4. *Prospector* will take lunar photographs.

   _____

Paragraph Comprehension

Directions: Read the paragraph below and answer the following questions.

There are no astronauts on *Prospector*. It will not land on the moon. *Prospector* will travel around the moon for a year. It will study the moon. It will help answer questions about it. How did the moon form? Of what is it made? Could humans live there someday?

1. What is *Prospector*?

   a. a spacecraft

   b. a telescope

   c. a science lab

   d. another name for the moon

2. What will *Prospector* do?

   a. land on the moon

   b. take men to the moon

   c. travel around the moon

   d. crash on the moon

3. What do scientists want to know about the moon?

   a. what it is made of

   b. how it was formed

   c. if people could live there

   d. all of the above

4. How long will *Prospector* travel?

   a. three years

   b. one month

   c. about a week

   d. one year

5. For what will *Prospector* be used?

   a. to study the planets

   b. to study the moon

   c. to study the solar system

   d. to study the sun

Whole Story Comprehension

Directions: Read the story below and answer the questions on the following page.

Back to the Moon!

The rocket's engines began to roar. People on the ground cheered as it blasted off. "We're on our way!" said scientist Scott Hubbard.

A small spacecraft called *Lunar Prospector* was inside the rocket's nose. An hour later, the spacecraft broke free and began a trip to the moon.

The U.S. space agency NASA sent a mission to the moon in 1972. "It feels good to be going back," said the scientist Joseph Boyce.

There are no astronauts on *Prospector*. It will not land on the moon. *Prospector* will travel around the moon for a year. It will study the moon. It will help answer questions about it. How did the moon form? Of what is it made? Could humans live there someday?

Prospector has tools to make a map of the moon. Other tools will study what the moon is made of.

Scientists think *Prospector* may find ice on the moon. A water supply on the moon could make it possible for people to live there.

Air would also be needed. But with the right equipment, people can live in strange places. "Today's kids may end up living on the moon," says Boyce.

Whole Story Comprehension *(cont.)*

Directions: After you have read the story on the previous page, answer the questions below.

1. Why did the people cheer?

    a. They were watching a race.

    b. The rocket blasted off.

    c. They saw the astronauts.

    d. a and b

2. At blastoff, where was the *Prospector*?

    a. in the nose of the rocket

    b. in the tail of the rocket

    c. in the center of the rocket

    d. none of the above

3. Why do you think there were no astronauts on *Prospector*?

    a. They were afraid to go.

    b. *Prospector* is too small to hold them.

    c. It is a dangerous spacecraft.

    d. none of the above

4. What do scientists think they might find on the moon?

    a. people

    b. plants

    c. ice

    d. lakes

5. What would people need in order to live on the moon?

    a. cars and houses

    b. rivers and mountains

    c. water and air

    d. stores and electricity

6. What will *Prospector's* tools do?

    a. make a map of the moon

    b. study what the moon is made of

    c. look for air on the moon

    d. a and b

7. Where might people live someday?

    a. on the sun

    b. on another planet

    c. on the moon

    d. none of the above

8. Before *Prospector*, when was the last moon mission?

    a. 1972

    b. 1967

    c. 1999

    d. 2000

Enrichment

Directions: Read the information below and then complete the activity.

The word *spacecraft* is a compound word.

The words *space* and *craft* are put together to make one word.

Choose a word from the first column and match it to a word in the second column. Put each set of words together to make a compound word. Write each word on the line.

space	bow
hall	book
school	rise
note	ship
sun	house
rain	way

1. _____

2. _____

3. _____

4. _____

5. _____

6. _____

Choose four more sets of words that can form compound words. First write them separately, and then combine them to form the compound word.

_____   _____   7. _____

_____   _____   8. _____

_____   _____   9. _____

_____   _____   10. _____

Graphic Development

Directions: Look at the pictures of the earth and the moon. Then answer "True" (T) or "False" (F).

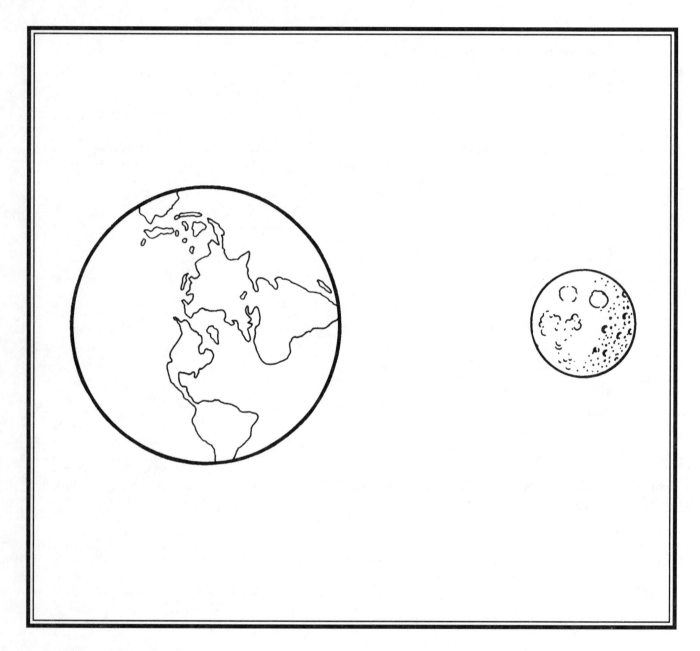

1. The moon is larger than the earth. _____

2. The moon has craters. _____

3. The earth has land and water. _____

4. The earth has many moons. _____

5. The earth only has one moon. _____

Sentence Comprehension

Directions: Read the following sentences carefully and answer the questions below "True" (T) or "False" (F).

Ten years ago, Engine Company 16 was a place for crime. After an emergency, firefighters returned to find smashed windows and missing equipment.

---

1. Engine Company 16 is a firehouse. _____

2. The firefighters broke the windows. _____

3. People destroyed the firehouse. _____

4. No one ever took their equipment. _____

5. The firehouse was a safe place. _____

Word Study

Directions: Use the words in the word bank to complete the sentences.

---

emergency   firefighter   crime   safe   homework

---

1. A person who fights fires is a _____.

2. School work that is done at home is _____.

3. Something that is against the law is a _____.

4. Another word for *accident* could be _____.

5. If you are protected, you are _____.

Paragraph Comprehension

Directions: Read the paragraph below and answer the following questions.

Nine-year-old Jeremy Woods drops by to play football. He stands on the fire truck.
"They tell me to stay away from drugs and to stay in school," he says. "It's my favorite
place to come."

1. Where does Jeremy come to visit?

    a. the park

    b. the firehouse

    c. the school

    d. the football field

2. Jeremy is probably in

    a. third grade.

    b. kindergarten.

    c. high school.

    d. college.

3. Why do you think Jeremy likes to visit?

    a. It's fun.

    b. There are things to do.

    c. People care about him.

    d. all of the above

4. Who tells Jeremy to stay away from drugs?

    a. his friends

    b. his neighbors

    c. the firefighters

    d. no one

5. Why do the firefighters tell Jeremy to stay in school?

    a. because it's boring

    b. so he won't be at home alone

    c. so he'll get a good education

    d. all of the above

Whole Story Comprehension

Directions: Read the story below and answer the questions on the following page.

The Friendliest Firehouse

Ten years ago, Engine Company 16 was a place for crime. After an emergency, firefighters returned to find smashed windows and missing equipment. They were frustrated. So, they just quit locking up. Soon, students from a nearby school began to visit. They used the bathroom, got their bikes fixed, or just hung out.

There was one problem. The kids were visiting during school hours. Arthur Lewis came up with an idea. With extra cash from the firehouse pay phone, he bought a few small radios. Kids who improved school attendance would win a radio. Later, the firefighters gave away bikes. They built them from donated parts. Result? Last year, Hartigan Elementary School's attendance rate shot up to 94%. That is one of the best rates in Chicago.

The men knew they could do even more for the kids. One man teaches chess. Another man cuts kids' hair. And another helps with math homework. Other firefighters collect winter clothes for the kids. Some have started baseball and basketball teams. Many of the men are there even when they aren't working. Engine Company 16 has really changed. It is now a safe place for hundreds of kids.

Nine-year-old Jeremy Woods drops by to play football. He stands on the fire truck. "They tell me to stay away from drugs and to stay in school," he says. "It's my favorite place to come."

Whole Story Comprehension (cont.)

Directions: After you have read the story on the previous page, answer the questions below.

1. *Frustrated* means

   a. disappointed.

   b. happy.

   c. ruined.

   d. on time.

2. When the kids started to visit, what was the problem?

   a. They were rude.

   b. They were fighting.

   c. They were skipping school.

   d. They wouldn't go home.

3. How did the kids win radios?

   a. by going to school

   b. by doing work

   c. by helping the firefighters

   d. by entering contests

4. Where is Hartigan Elementary School?

   a. Phoenix, Arizona

   b. Austin, Texas

   c. Chicago, Illinois

   d. New York, New York

5. Why do you think the firefighters wanted to spend time with kids?

   a. They were bored.

   b. They didn't have anything better to do.

   c. They wanted to help them.

   d. They wished they had their own kids.

6. What sports do the kids play?

   a. baseball and soccer

   b. basketball and hockey

   c. baseball, basketball, and football

   d. tennis and volleyball

7. The firefighters probably give the children winter clothes because

   a. they don't have a lot of money.

   b. they don't have any stores nearby.

   c. they don't like to buy their own clothes.

   d. none of the above

8. How many kids visit the firehouse now?

   a. about 10

   b. less than 50

   c. more than 100

   d. more than 1,000

Enrichment

Directions: Write the two words that make up each compound word.

1. firefighter   = _____ + _____

2. baseball   = _____ + _____

3. basketball   = _____ + _____

4. football   = _____ + _____

5. homework   = _____ + _____

6. bathroom   = _____ + _____

Now think of four more compound words. First write the compound word, then write the two words that make up each compound word.

7. _____ = _____ + _____

8. _____ = _____ + _____

9. _____ = _____ + _____

10. _____ = _____ + _____

Graphic Development

Directions: Complete the web about the story.

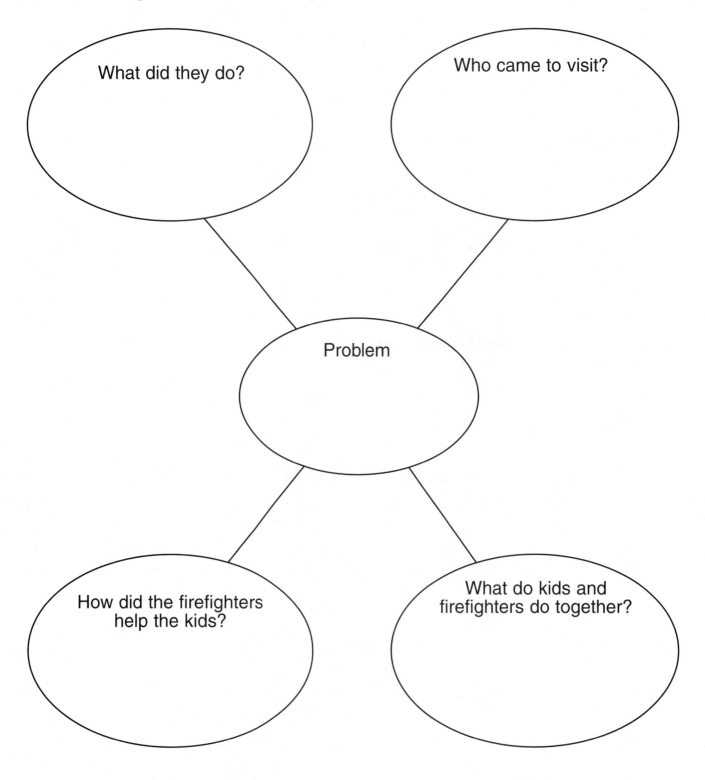

What did they do?

Who came to visit?

Problem

How did the firefighters help the kids?

What do kids and firefighters do together?

Sentence Comprehension

Directions: Read the following sentences carefully and answer the questions below "True" (T) or "False" (F).

Why was a fourth grade class out in the marsh? To help save crabs, birds, and fish!

1. High-school kids were in the marsh. _____

2. The fourth graders were destroying the marsh. _____

3. A marsh is outdoors. _____

4. The kids were being helpful. _____

5. Animals will be helped by the children. _____

Word Study

Directions: Read the definitions. Then write the word that best completes each sentence.

marsh
an area of soft, wet land
estuary
an area where ocean water meets river water

1. Fish live in the _____.

2. Raccoons walked through the _____.

3. Tall grasses grow in the _____.

4. It is important to keep the water in the _____ clean.

Paragraph Comprehension

Directions: Read the paragraph below and answer the following questions.

> The Silver Bay School is in Toms River, New Jersey. It is beside the Barnegat Bay estuary. An estuary is an area where ocean water mixes with river water. Many plants and animals grow well there. But the estuary is polluted. Animals are dying.

1. An estuary is

   a. an area of water.

   b. an area of land.

   c. a building.

   d. a wall.

2. Who lives in the estuary?

   a. people

   b. plants

   c. animals

   d. both b and c

3. Toms River is probably

   a. in the forest.

   b. in the mountains.

   c. near the ocean.

   d. in the desert.

4. The problem with Barnegat Bay estuary is

   a. pollution.

   b. lack of water.

   c. dirty air.

   d. too many people.

5. If the area is not cleaned up, what will happen?

   a. It will be ugly.

   b. No one will visit.

   c. Animals will die.

   d. all of the above

Whole Story Comprehension

Directions: Read the story below and answer the questions on the following page.

Marching Through the Marsh

Why was a fourth grade class out in the marsh? To help save crabs, birds, and fish!

The Silver Bay School is in Toms River, New Jersey. It is beside the Barnegat Bay estuary. An estuary is an area where ocean water mixes with river water. Many plants and animals grow well there. But the estuary is polluted. Animals are dying.

The 25 students wrote letters to the township committee. Mark Mutter is the head of parks and recreation. He came to their class to talk about the estuary's food chain. They learned about the animals that grow and feed there. Many of these animals are being hurt by pollution. The students decided to clean up the estuary to help.

They went to the Cattus Island County Park. They walked to the salt marsh. They carried garbage bags. The students picked up bottles and leaves. They even found a mattress floating in the water. "I learned you can save an animal just by picking up a piece of trash," said one girl. "The animal's beak can get stuck in a soda bottle or piece of plastic."

After cleaning up the marsh, the class decided to start a new project. They wanted to get the whole town involved. They called it "Save the Bays and Waterways."

The kids learned that one person can make a difference. People who see the sparkling bay as they drive along the shore can learn that lesson, too.

Whole Story Comprehension (cont.)

Directions: After you have read the story on the previous page, answer the questions below.

1. Who wanted to save the marsh?

   a. visitors

   b. teachers

   c. children

   d. the mayor

2. How did the children help?

   a. They complained about the trash.

   b. They picked up the trash.

   c. They moved away.

   d. They read books about pollution.

3. What can kill animals and plants?

   a. pollution

   b. too much sunshine

   c. too much rain

   d. ocean water

4. What is pollution?

   a. trash

   b. dirty air

   c. dirty water

   d. all of the above

5. Why did the children go to the park?

   a. to clean up

   b. to take pictures

   c. to learn about the marsh

   d. to see the beautiful water

6. To whom did the children write letters?

   a. their parents

   b. their neighbors

   c. the township committee

   d. kids at school

7. The kids in the story learned that
   _____ can make a difference.

   a. a group of people

   b. lots of people working together

   c. one person

   d. adults

8. The kids will help even more by

   a. getting the town involved.

   b. inviting people to visit.

   c. staying away from the marsh.

   d. all of the above

Enrichment

Directions: Read the information below and complete the activity.

When two words have the same ending sound, they are called **rhyming words**.

Here are some examples:

bays ways

car far

Write a rhyming word for each word below.

1. sky   _____

2. house   _____

3. sea   _____

4. clean   _____

The children in Toms River started a project called "Save the Bays and Waterways." The words *Bays* and *Waterways* rhyme. Write another rhyming name for their project.

_____

Graphic Development

Directions: Label the picture to show where each animal lives.

bluefish	hawks	raccoons
crabs	blue herons (birds)	

Sentence Comprehension

Directions: Read the following sentences carefully and answer the questions below "True" (T) or "False" (F).

Jupiter is the king of planets. It is the biggest in our solar system.

1. Jupiter is the king of a country. _____

2. There are many planets in our solar system. _____

3. Jupiter is large. _____

4. Jupiter is close to Earth. _____

5. Earth is larger than Jupiter. _____

Word Study

Directions: Read the information below and answer the question.

Jupiter is the name of a Roman god. He was the god of light. He was the god of the sky. He was the god of weather.

Why do you think the planet Jupiter was given this name?

_____

_____

_____

_____

Paragraph Comprehension

Directions: Read the paragraph below and answer the following questions.

Jupiter has rings. You can see Saturn's rings through a telescope. But the rings around Jupiter are very hard to see.

1. What is hard to see on Jupiter?

    a. its colors

    b. its size

    c. its rings

    d. none of the above

2. Which planet has rings that can easily be seen?

    a. Saturn

    b. Jupiter

    c. Earth

    d. a and c

3. Why is a telescope used?

    a. to look at very small things

    b. to look inside things

    c. to see inside the body

    d. to see things that are far away

4. Can scientists see Jupiter's rings?

    a. yes

    b. no

    c. not sure

    d. Jupiter doesn't have rings.

5. How are Jupiter and Saturn the same?

    a. They are the same color.

    b. They both have rings.

    c. They are the same size.

    d. none of the above

Whole Story Comprehension

Directions: Read the story below and answer the questions on the following page.

Rings Around Jupiter

Jupiter is the king of planets. It is the biggest in our solar system. There is a storm on Jupiter. It is called the Great Red Spot. You can see it with a telescope. This storm is twice as big as Earth!

Jupiter has rings. You can see Saturn's rings through a telescope. But the rings around Jupiter are very hard to see.

In 1998, scientists made a great discovery. They were studying 36 new pictures of Jupiter taken in space. They figured out how its rings are formed. Jupiter's rings are thin layers of moon dust.

Jupiter has very strong gravity (grav-i-tee). That is the force that keeps us from flying into space. Jupiter's gravity pulls comets and space rocks toward it. Some of the rocks crash into Jupiter's moons. The crash makes a big cloud of dust. The dust flies into space. Then it goes into orbit and helps form a ring.

In thousands of years, the little moons will disappear. All that will be left of them is Jupiter's dusty rings. "That could never happen to Earth's moon," says space scientist Maureen Ockert-Bell. "Our moon is just too big."

Whole Story Comprehension *(cont.)*

Directions: After you have read the story on the previous page, answer the questions below.

1. What is Jupiter's nickname?

    a. King of the Sky

    b. King of Planets

    c. Biggest of Planets

    d. The Bright Planet

2. What is the Great Red Spot?

    a. a storm

    b. a crater

    c. a ring

    d. a moon

3. Of what are Jupiter's rings made?

    a. stars

    b. moons

    c. moon dust

    d. b and c

4. What force keeps us on the ground?

    a. weight

    b. balance

    c. gravity

    d. strength

5. What is orbit?

    a. a path around something

    b. the name of a planet

    c. when two moons crash

    d. moon dust

6. What will happen to Jupiter's moons someday?

    a. They will get bigger.

    b. They will disappear.

    c. They will change color.

    d. They will become planets.

7. Why won't Earth's moon break apart?

    a. It is too big.

    b. It is stronger.

    c. Nothing will hit it.

    d. It is too far away.

8. Why does Jupiter pull comets and space rocks toward it?

    a. It needs to become bigger.

    b. It has strong gravity.

    c. It needs to have rings.

    d. all of the above

Enrichment

Directions: Read the information below. Complete the activity.

The word *gravity* is pronounced grav-i-tee. Sometimes words are hard to pronounce. Authors and dictionaries use different spellings to help the reader pronounce words.

Read each pronunciation and write the word using the correct spelling.

1. Ju-pet-er _____

2. sis-tem _____

3. Sa-tern _____

4. dis-kover-ee _____

Think of four more difficult to pronounce words and write the different spellings to help you pronounce them.

5. _____   _____

6. _____   _____

7. _____   _____

8. _____   _____

Graphic Development

Directions: Complete the web with information about Jupiter. Fill in topics for each oval and then write the information you know about each topic.

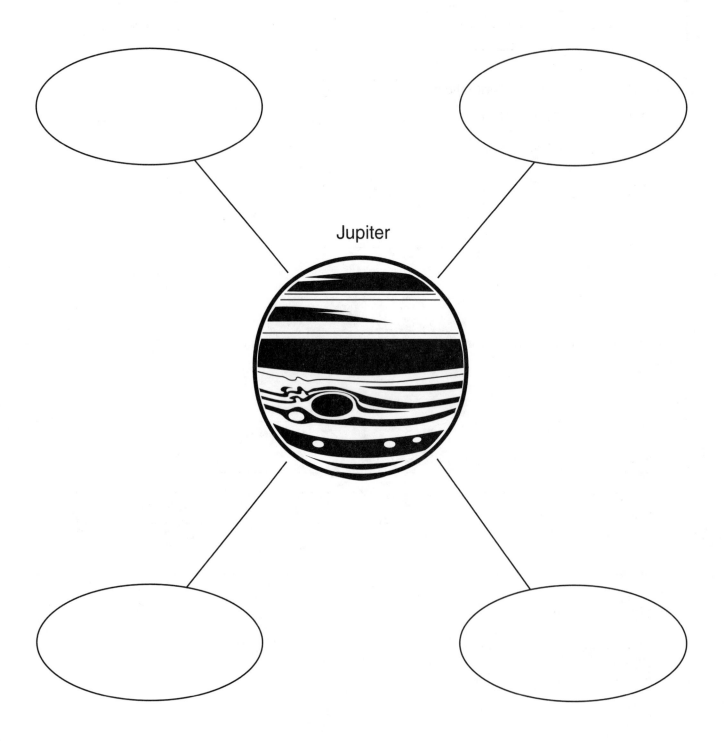

Jupiter

Sentence Comprehension

Directions: Read the following sentence carefully and answer the questions below "True" (T) or "False" (F).

I would like to see our nation's rivers cleaned up so that we have clean drinking water and a great place to fish.

1. Some rivers are polluted. _____

2. It is not safe to drink polluted water. _____

3. All rivers are clean. _____

4. People can clean up a dirty river. _____

5. Healthy fish live in polluted rivers. _____

Word Study

Directions: Read the information below. Then write "F" if the sentence is a fact or "O" if it is an opinion.

A **fact** is something that is always true.

An **opinion** is how you feel about something. People write letters to the editor when they want to tell their opinions.

1. Fish live in rivers. _____

2. Rivers are beautiful. _____

3. I love to swim. _____

4. People sometimes pollute rivers. _____

5. Fishing is fun. _____

6. A river trip is a great vacation. _____

Paragraph Comprehension

Directions: Read the paragraph below and answer the following questions.

Have you ever been boating on a river? You would expect to see clear water, fish, birds, and healthy plants. Let me tell you about my trip down our local river.

1. This story is about a

    a. holiday.

    b. television show.

    c. river trip.

    d. storm.

2. Rivers should have

    a. clear water.

    b. fish.

    c. healthy plants.

    d. all of the above

3. On river trips, people probably

    a. fish.

    b. sleep.

    c. play sports.

    d. watch movies.

4. The word *local* means

    a. nearby.

    b. out of state.

    c. in another country.

    d. none of the above

5. Which of the following is bad for wildlife?

    a. sunshine

    b. pollution

    c. plants

    d. rain

Whole Story Comprehension

Directions: Read the letter below and answer the questions on the following page.

Save Our Streams

Dear Editor,

Have you ever been boating on a river? You would expect to see clear water, fish, birds, and healthy plants. Let me tell you about my trip down our local river.

I saw a refrigerator, a dead cow, and soda pop cans. I also saw plastic cups, sewer pipes, and dirty water. I didn't enjoy this trip. There is so much pollution in the river.

I would like to see our nation's rivers cleaned up so that we have clean drinking water and a great place to fish. Trash and waste products need to be removed. Maybe our laws could be more strict. Then people would think before they polluted our waterways.

When I grow up and bring my son down the river, I want him to see only fish, birds, clean water, and green plants. Wouldn't it be nice if he could also take a drink?

Sincerely,

Matthew Raborn, 10

Our Lady of Fatima School

Lafayette, Louisiana

Whole Story Comprehension *(cont.)*

Directions: After you have read the previous page, answer the questions below.

1. Which of the following does not belong in a river?

   a. fish

   b. soda pop cans

   c. plants

   d. all of the above

2. What does a sewer pipe do?

   a. It carries fresh water.

   b. It carries waste water.

   c. It drains a river.

   d. It cleans a river.

3. Who should be responsible for cleaning up pollution?

   a. the government

   b. adults

   c. children

   d. everyone

4. The word *strict* means

   a. easy.

   b. soft.

   c. harsh.

   d. relaxed.

5. Clean water helps

   a. people.

   b. fish.

   c. birds.

   d. all living things.

6. What things should you see on a river trip?

   a. fish and birds

   b. trash

   c. dirty water

   d. sewer pipes

7. The person who wrote this letter is

   a. a teenage girl.

   b. a young boy.

   c. a woman.

   d. a college boy.

8. An editor works for

   a. a school.

   b. the city.

   c. a newspaper.

   d. a church.

Enrichment

Directions: Read the information and complete the activity.

When a beginning letter sound is repeated in a sentence, it is called **alliteration**.

Here are some examples:

Save our streams.

Fifty fish fan their fins.

Pop cans, pipes, and plastic make pollution.

Write an alliterative sentence for each word below.

1. birds

_____

_____

2. water

_____

_____

3. river

_____

_____

Graphic Development

Directions: Write a letter to the editor about pollution in your community.

Sentence Comprehension

Directions: Read the following sentences carefully and answer the questions below "True" (T) or "False" (F).

> I'm talking about our new "improved" school cafeteria. It gives the choice between fast food and "regular" food.

1. *Improved* means better. _____

2. A cafeteria is a place that serves food. _____

3. Regular food is bad food. _____

4. Schools serve different kinds of food. _____

Word Study

Directions: Healthy food is good for your body. It gives your body what it needs to grow and be strong. Make a list of healthy foods and not-so-healthy foods using the word bank below.

fruit
chicken
chips
candy
French fries
milk
salad
soda pop

Healthy	Not-So-Healthy

Paragraph Comprehension

Directions: Read the paragraph below and answer the following questions.

Cafeteria food was never very good. But they tried to offer a balanced diet. Somebody out there was trying to make us eat our vegetables. A lot of us didn't like it, so we brought our own peanut butter sandwiches, instead.

1. This author
    a. likes cafeteria food.
    b. doesn't like cafeteria food.
    c. wants to be a cafeteria cook.
    d. b and c

2. A balanced diet means eating
    a. a mix of different healthy foods.
    b. a lot of meat.
    c. only fruit and vegetables.
    d. and exercising every day.

3. Why would a cafeteria serve vegetables to kids?
    a. so they will eat healthy food
    b. because they hate vegetables
    c. because most kids love vegetables
    d. because they don't cost very much

4. What can students do if they don't like cafeteria lunches?
    a. go to a restaurant
    b. skip eating lunch
    c. bring a lunch from home
    d. none of the above

5. Which of the following would not be included in a healthy diet?
    a. milk
    b. fruit
    c. chocolate
    d. meat

Whole Story Comprehension

Directions: Read the story below and answer the questions on the following page.

Food for Thought

Freedom of choice is not always a good thing. It's great to be able to choose a movie. Also, it's fun to choose the clothes you wear. But there are some things that are just too important to be left up to students. I'm talking about our new "improved" school cafeteria. It gives the choice between fast food and "regular" food.

Cafeteria food was never very good. But the school tried to offer a balanced diet. Somebody out there was trying to make us eat our vegetables. A lot of us didn't like it, so we brought our own peanut butter sandwiches, instead.

How do you make kids eat cafeteria food? There are two ways. My school chose the wrong one. First, you can make the food better. You can make it healthy, tasty, and fresh. Second, you can serve food you know kids will eat, even if it's not good for them.

That's exactly what happened at our school. A week after the new fast-food counter opened, most of our students were ordering fries and shakes for lunch.

This is not a healthy choice. Half of the people in our country are overweight. We should be learning about good food and good eating habits. Above all, we should be learning that good food does not have to taste bad.

Whole Story Comprehension (cont.)

Directions: After you have read the story on the previous page, answer the questions below.

1. The author of this story thinks that

    a. fast food is healthy.

    b. cafeterias should serve healthy food.

    c. kids should bring their own lunches to school.

    d. vegetables taste bad.

2. A lunch of fries and shakes

    a. is healthy.

    b. is unhealthy.

    c. doesn't really matter.

    d. none of the above

3. Half of the people in our country

    a. are overweight.

    b. hate vegetables.

    c. love chocolate.

    d. exercise every day.

4. This author believes that cafeterias should serve

    a. food kids like.

    b. healthier foods.

    c. desserts.

    d. more pizza.

5. Which of the following makes the healthiest lunch?

    a. fries and a shake

    b. an apple and a tomato

    c. chicken sandwich, milk, and an orange

    d. pizza, soda, and a cookie

6. The author believes that schools should teach kids

    a. good eating habits.

    b. how to behave at lunchtime.

    c. how to earn money for their lunches.

    d. none of the above

7. Which of the following is false?

    a. Too much fat is bad for you.

    b. Healthy food tastes bad.

    c. It is good to eat vegetables.

    d. People should drink water every day.

8. Why did the school serve fast food?

    a. Kids weren't buying the other food.

    b. It is healthier for them.

    c. It costs less to make.

    d. a and b

Enrichment

Directions: Read the information below and complete the activity.

An author uses a "voice" when writing. The author of the article you read on page 111 uses a voice that is not happy. The author tells the things he or she doesn't like using strong opinions.

Write a sentence about cafeteria food for each voice below.

1. pleased

   _____

   _____

2. angry

   _____

   _____

3. excited

   _____

   _____

4. unsure

   _____

   _____

Graphic Development

Directions: Write or draw pictures of foods in each section of the food pyramid.

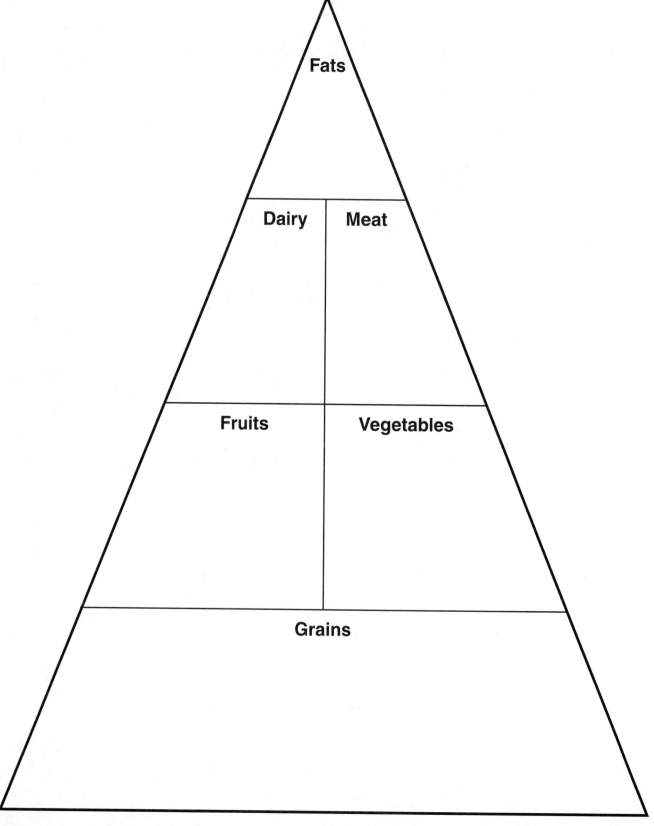

Sentence Comprehension

Directions: Read the following sentence carefully and answer the questions below "True" (T) or "False" (F).

> The teen smoking rate has gone up since the early 1990s.

1. Some teenagers smoke. _____

2. More teenagers smoke now than they used to. _____

3. All teens smoke cigarettes. _____

4. It is bad to smoke cigarettes. _____

5. Smoking is unhealthy. _____

Word Study

Directions: Read the definitions below and complete the activity.

> **lung**
>
> an organ in the body used for breathing
>
> **damage**
>
> harm caused

Smoking causes lung damage in all people. It is especially harmful to kids. Write about the meaning of lung damage and how smoking can cause it.

_____

_____

_____

_____

_____

Paragraph Comprehension

Directions: Read the paragraph below and answer the following questions.

It is important to keep kids from smoking. There was a study done with kids who smoke every day. It shows that these kids get lung damage. The body can never fix it.

1. If kids smoke, they can
   a. grow old quickly.
   b. get lung damage.
   c. be healthier.
   d. a and b

2. A study is like a
   a. book.
   b. movie.
   c. test.
   d. game.

3. The body can never fix
   a. lung damage.
   b. a broken bone.
   c. sickness.
   d. a cold.

4. If you have lung damage, you can have trouble
   a. breathing.
   b. sleeping.
   c. growing.
   d. reading.

5. Who do you think studies kids and smoking?
   a. parents
   b. teachers
   c. scientists
   d. none of the above

Whole Story Comprehension

Directions: Read the story below and answer the questions on the following page.

Florida Kids Crush Out Smoking

What can a state get for $70 million? Florida spent it on ads against smoking. The ads were made mostly by kids. Result? The teen smoking rate made a big drop in just one year!

The teen smoking rate has gone up since the early 1990s. About three million teens smoke. In 1996, Florida won $13 billion. They got it from a lawsuit against tobacco companies. They wanted to use part of the money to stop kids from smoking. They let kids think up ideas for the ads.

It is important to keep kids from smoking. There was a study done with kids who smoke every day. It shows that these kids get lung damage. The body can never fix it.

"It didn't matter if [kids] were heavy or light smokers. What mattered was that they started young," said scientist John K. Wiencke. Thank goodness that in Florida, people who are against smoking are starting young, too!

Whole Story Comprehension (cont.)

Directions: After you have read the story on the previous page, answer the questions below.

1. How much money was spent on no smoking ads?

    a. $7,000

    b. $70,000

    c. $70 billion

    d. $70 million

2. What happened after the ads were used?

    a. More teenagers started smoking.

    b. Fewer kids were smoking.

    c. Many kids had lung damage.

    d. Nothing happened.

3. How did Florida get the money?

    a. from a lawsuit

    b. from donations

    c. found it

    d. borrowed it from a bank

4. Who came up with the ad ideas?

    a. the law makers

    b. teachers

    c. families

    d. kids

5. What is the most important reason not to smoke?

    a. It can make you sick.

    b. It makes you smell bad.

    c. It is expensive.

    d. It gives you bad breath.

6. Whom did scientists study?

    a. teenagers who smoke sometimes

    b. kids who smoke every day

    c. adults who smoke

    d. people who live with smokers

7. What can smoking cause?

    a. health problems

    b. lung damage

    c. trouble breathing

    d. all of the above

8. What do you think would happen if Florida put out more no smoking ads?

    a. The smoking rate would drop more.

    b. No one would pay attention.

    c. More kids would start smoking.

    d. Nothing would happen.

Enrichment

Directions: Read the information below and complete the activity.

Graphs are used to show information. You can graph the kinds of pets your friends have or how many kids in your class are buying lunch.

Decide on a topic and complete the graph below.

Title of Graph

Graphic Development

Directions: Use the graph to answer the questions.

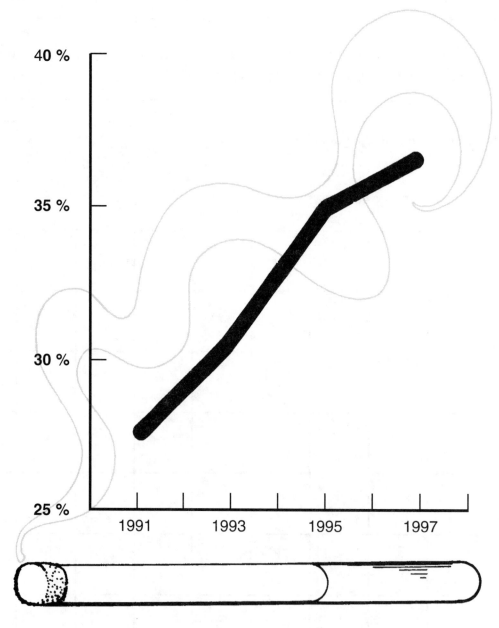

1. About what percent of teens smoked in 1991? _____

2. Did more teens smoke in 1993 or 1997?_____

3. Do you think teens smoked more or less in 1990 than in 1991? _____

4. The smoking rate did not grow as quickly between 1995 and 1997. Why do you think that is?

    _____

    _____

Sentence Comprehension

Directions: Read the following sentences carefully and answer the questions below "True" (T) or "False" (F).

> The floods have killed people. Now a new dam will stop these floods. It will also create electricity.

1. A dam can stop flooding. _____

2. Floods are dangerous. _____

3. Floods create electricity. _____

4. Dams can be helpful. _____

5. A dam holds back water. _____

Word Study

Directions: Read the definition below and answer the questions.

> **dam**
>
> A dam holds back water. It keeps a river from flowing out of control. When a dam is made, a lake is formed.

1. How can a dam be helpful?

   _____

   _____

   _____

2. How might a dam change the environment in a bad way?

   _____

   _____

   _____

Paragraph Comprehension

Directions: Read the paragraph below and answer the following questions.

In 1997, China took a big step with the river. They dumped rocks into parts of it. They were getting ready to build a dam. It will be completed in 2009. It will be the biggest in the world. It will stop flooding. It will turn the water's energy into electricity.

1. How long will it take to build the dam?

   a. one year

   b. three years

   c. more than 10 years

   d. more than 20 years

2. Why were rocks dumped into the river?

   a. to start building the dam

   b. to finish the dam

   c. to clean them

   d. a and c

3. What will the dam do?

   a. stop flooding

   b. make electricity

   c. both a and b

   d. none of the above

4. Where is this dam being built?

   a. in the United States

   b. in Australia

   c. in China

   d. in Japan

5. The dam will be

   a. the biggest in the world.

   b. just a small dam.

   c. dangerous to the people.

   d. none of the above

Whole Story Comprehension

Directions: Read the story below and answer the questions on the following page.

China's Dam is a Good Idea

China's Yangtze River is beautiful. But the river floods. The floods have killed many people. Now a new dam will stop these floods. It will also create electricity.

In 1997, China took a big step with the river. They dumped rocks into parts of it. They were getting ready to build a dam. It will be completed in 2009. It will be the biggest in the world. It will stop flooding. It will turn the water's energy into electricity.

Some people don't want the dam. A long lake will be formed by it. It will swallow up villages. Millions of people must move. The dam will destroy the homes of giant pandas, river dolphins, and other rare animals.

Still, the dam will do more good than harm. More electricity will help make new businesses. The people who must move are the ones put in danger by the floods. Some wildlife habitats will be destroyed, but many more will stay. Progress often causes problems. The Three Gorges Dam is a great example of progress!

Whole Story Comprehension *(cont.)*

Directions: After you have read the story on the previous page, answer the questions below.

1. Which of the following is not true about the Yangtze River?

    a. It is beautiful.

    b. It is in China.

    c. It floods.

    d. It makes electricity.

2. Why don't some people want the dam built?

    a. They will lose their homes.

    b. It will destroy animal habitats.

    c. It will destroy villages.

    d. all of the above

3. What does a dam do?

    a. It holds back water.

    b. It makes a river.

    c. It makes dangerous flooding.

    d. all of the above

4. What else can this dam do?

    a. It can dry up the land.

    b. It can make electricity.

    c. It can be a home for beavers.

    d. none of the above

5. Giant pandas and river dolphins are

    a. rare animals.

    b. extinct.

    c. being moved to other parts of the world.

    d. none of the above

6. More electricity will help

    a. the animals.

    b. the people by the river.

    c. businesses.

    d. no one.

7. A *habitat* is

    a. a kind of clothing.

    b. a place where an animal lives.

    c. a kind of dam.

    d. a lot of money.

8. *Progress* means

    a. moving ahead.

    b. doing nothing.

    c. destroying things.

    d. taking turns.

Enrichment

Directions: Read the information and complete the activity.

Commas are used in sentences to separate listed items.

Here is an example:

The dam will destroy the homes of giant pandas, river dolphins, and other rare animals.

Add commas to the sentences below. Rewrite each sentence with the commas in the correct places.

1. People villages and animals are near the river.

    _____

    _____

2. The dam will stop flooding keep people safe and make electricity.

    _____

    _____

3. Building a dam takes time hard work and money.

    _____

    _____

4. More electricity will help people businesses and towns.

    _____

    _____

Graphic Development

Directions: Use the map to answer the questions.

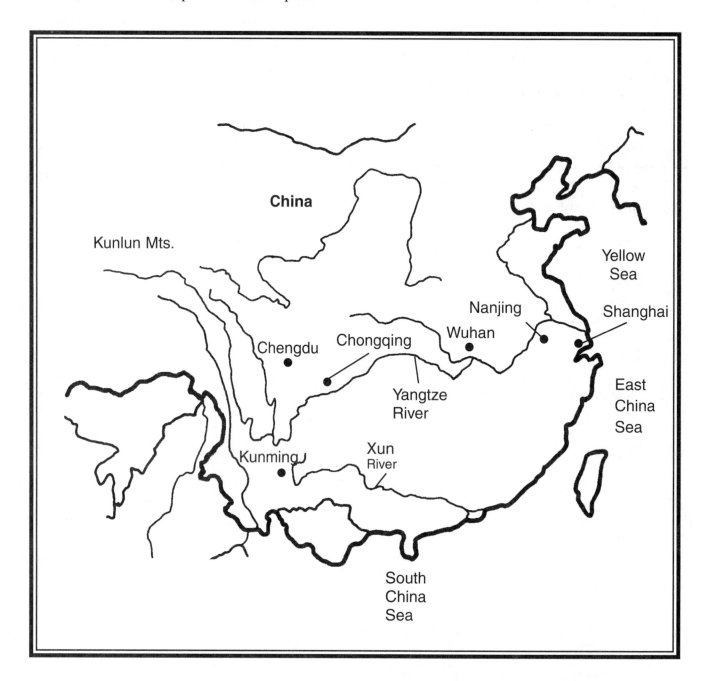

1. The Yangtze River begins in what mountains? _____

2. The Yangtze River ends in what city? _____

3. The Yangtze River flows into which sea? _____

4. Name two towns that are very close to the river. _____

Sentence Comprehension

Directions: Read the following sentences carefully and answer the questions below "True" (T) or "False" (F).

Tibet is in China. It has a rich history and culture.

---

1. Tibet is a part of China. _____

2. Tibet is bigger than China. _____

3. People live in Tibet. _____

4. People have lived in Tibet for a long time. _____

Word Study

Directions: Read the definitions and complete the activity.

---

history

important events of the past

culture

traditions, customs, way of life

Write about your family history and culture.

_____

_____

_____

_____

_____

_____

_____

_____

_____

Paragraph Comprehension

Directions: Read the paragraph below and answer the following questions.

> Tibet is in China. It has a rich history and culture. But the Chinese do not let the people fly their flag. They are not allowed to practice their religion. Tibet's leader has lived in India for 30 years. He is working to free Tibet. But, he says, "There has been no change."

1. The people of Tibet cannot

   a. fly their own flag.

   b. practice their own religion.

   c. own farms.

   d. both a and b

2. Tibet's leader lives in

   a. China.

   b. Tibet.

   c. India.

   d. no one knows

3. What is the leader trying to do?

   a. make a new flag

   b. go back to Tibet

   c. free his people

   d. become the leader of India

4. How long has the leader lived in India?

   a. one year

   b. 10 years

   c. 30 years

   d. 40 years

5. How successful has the leader been with freeing his people?

   a. There has been no change.

   b. He is making a big difference.

   c. The Chinese people are starting to change.

   d. none of the above

Whole Story Comprehension

Directions: Read the story below and answer the questions on the following page.

A Dangerous Road to Freedom

Tibet is in China. It has a rich history and culture. But the Chinese do not let the people fly their flag. They are not allowed to practice their religion. Tibet's leader has lived in India for 30 years. He is working to free Tibet. But, he says, "There has been no change."

Many people in Tibet have moved to India. Most go to India in the winter. There are less Chinese police at the border. Some die on the trip.

In India, kids from Tibet can study their language and religion. But they miss their families. Most live in crowded foster homes. They sleep two or three kids to a bed.

Parents say this is better than living in China. But when the children finish school, there are few jobs for them in India.

Sonam Tsering, 17, has lived in India for 10 years. He dreams of a free Tibet: "Then I will return to develop my country and build a good life."

Whole Story Comprehension (cont.)

Directions: After you have read the story on the previous page, answer the questions below.

1. Tibet is in

   a. Asia.

   b. Europe.

   c. North America.

   d. Australia.

2. When do most people try to leave Tibet?

   a. in the summer

   b. in the spring

   c. in the winter

   d. in the daytime

3. Where do the Tibetan children stay in India?

   a. with the leader

   b. in tents

   c. in foster homes

   d. in hospitals

4. What are the children able to do in India?

   a. study language and religion

   b. work

   c. live with their own families

   d. none of the above

5. Why do parents send their children to India?

   a. They can't afford to feed them.

   b. They like India.

   c. They think it is better than China.

   d. They don't want them anymore.

6. What often happens when the children finish school?

   a. They go back to Tibet.

   b. They can't find jobs.

   c. They try to escape.

   d. They become teachers.

7. Why do so many children share the same beds?

   a. They need to keep warm.

   b. They are afraid to be alone.

   c. They don't have enough space for everyone.

   d. a and c

8. Why does Sonam want to return to Tibet?

   a. He doesn't like India.

   b. He is afraid in India.

   c. He doesn't know anyone in India.

   d. He believes China will be better someday.

Enrichment

Directions: Read the information and complete the activity.

Adjectives are words that describe nouns. Adjectives help the reader to picture what is written.

Compare the sentences below.

Many people in Tibet have moved to India.

*Many **unhappy** people in Tibet have moved to India.*

*The word **unhappy** describes the people.*

Rewrite each sentence below, adding at least one adjective.

1. The leader is working to free Tibet.

_____

_____

2. Most go to India in the winter.

_____

_____

3. They sleep two or three kids to a bed.

_____

_____

4. Parents say this is better than living in China.

_____

_____

Graphic Development

Directions: Look at the map key. Use the map to answer the questions.

1. What are the names of two mountains shown on the map? _____

2. How many lakes are shown on the map? _____

3. Which city is closest to India? _____

4. Which city is closest to Lake Namco? _____

Sentence Comprehension

Directions: Read the following sentences carefully and answer the questions below "True" (T) or "False" (F).

> For hundreds of years, wolves roamed the West. But when white settlers came in the 1800s, they feared them.

1. Wolves have not been in the West for long. _____

2. White settlers were afraid of the wolves. _____

3. Wolves have always been kept in cages. _____

4. Hundreds of years ago, people kept wolves as pets. _____

5. Wolves are wild animals. _____

Word Study

Directions: Read the information below and answer the question.

> **Yellowstone National Park**
>
> Yellowstone was named a national park on March 1, 1872. It was set apart as a public park for the enjoyment of the people. The park was to be left in its natural condition. Yellowstone is the first and oldest national park in the world.

Think about the living and nonliving things that can be found in a wilderness area. How does making an area a national park help to keep it safe?

_____

_____

_____

_____

_____

Paragraph Comprehension

Directions: Read the paragraph below and answer the following questions.

Killing wolves had a big effect on the animals and plants. Wolves hunt coyotes and elk. With the wolves gone, these animals grew in numbers. Plants that are eaten by elk began to disappear. The government decided to bring wolves back to Yellowstone. It trapped some in Canada. The wolves were moved to the park. The goal: to put nature back in balance.

---

1. What did the wolves hunt?

   a. plants

   b. elk

   c. coyote

   d. both b and c

2. What happened to the elk when the wolves were gone?

   a. They died.

   b. They left the area.

   c. They ate all the plants.

   d. They got sick.

3. Who decided to bring the wolves back?

   a. the government

   b. farmers

   c. park visitors

   d. none of the above

4. Where did they find the wolves in order to bring them back?

   a. Yellowstone

   b. Canada

   c. in the park

   d. a zoo

5. What was out of balance when the wolves were gone?

   a. the people

   b. the country

   c. nature

   d. none of the above

Whole Story Comprehension

Directions: Read the story below and answer the questions on the following page.

The Wolf Packs Are Back

For hundreds of years, wolves roamed the West. But when white settlers came in the 1800s, they feared them. Wolves often killed sheep and cattle.

To help farmers, the government paid to kill wolves. By the early 1930s, all of the wolves in Yellowstone National Park were gone.

Killing the wolves had a big effect on the animals and plants. Coyotes and elk are hunted by wolves. With the wolves gone, these animals grew in numbers. Plants that are eaten by elk began to disappear. The government decided to bring wolves back to Yellowstone. It trapped some in Canada. The wolves were moved to the park. The goal: to put nature back into balance.

Not everyone was glad to see the wolves return. Farmers near the park were angry. The wolves have killed some sheep and cattle.

Some people think returning the wolves was against the law. A judge agreed with them. The judge said the wolves should be removed.

Many experts are fighting the judge's decision. The wolves have helped the park. Native plants are growing because there are fewer elk eating them. Beavers, which eat these plants, are also helped. Animals from the grizzly bear to the carrion beetle are doing well.

The wolves have a good friend named Bruce Babbitt. He is in charge of national parks. Babbitt says, "I will fight with everything I have to keep the wolves in Yellowstone." Anyone who cares about wildlife should join this fight.

Whole Story Comprehension *(cont.)*

Directions: After you have read the story on the previous page, answer the questions below.

1. Why didn't farmers like the wolves?

   a. They hurt people.

   b. They ate their crops.

   c. They killed their cattle.

   d. They ruined their property.

2. What did the government pay to have done?

   a. have the wolves killed

   b. move the wolves away

   c. protect the cattle

   d. put the wolves in a zoo

3. Why were the plants in the park disappearing?

   a. The wolves were eating them.

   b. There was no rain.

   c. The elk were eating them.

   d. The farmers took them.

4. How did the farmers feel about the return of the wolves?

   a. They were happy.

   b. They were afraid.

   c. They were angry.

   d. none of the above

5. Which animals do the wolves help?

   a. beavers

   b. sheep

   c. cattle

   d. none of the above

6. Who is fighting for the wolves?

   a. Bruce Babbitt

   b. a judge

   c. the government

   d. the farmers

7. What did the judge decide to do?

   a. keep the wolves in the park

   b. get rid of the wolves

   c. move the farmers

   d. move the park

8. Anyone who cares about wildlife should

   a. join the fight to keep the wolves.

   b. join the fight to get rid of the wolves.

   c. stay away from Yellowstone Park.

   d. all of the above

Enrichment

Directions: Read the information below and complete the activity.

Food Chain

The food chain is the order of different living things. Each one feeds on the one below it.

Think about the animals that live in your area. Draw pictures showing a food chain (example: wolves eat elk, elks eat plants, etc.).

Write about what would happen if one of the parts of the food chain were to be removed.

_____

_____

_____

_____

Graphic Development

Directions: There are many things to do at Yellowstone National Park. If you looked at a map of the park, you would find many symbols. Write what each symbol represents. Then answer the questions.

1.  _____

2.  _____

3.  _____

4.  _____

5.  _____

| boat |
| campground |
| horse |
| picnic area |
| store |

6. What are two things that you can do at the park? _____

7. Where can a person sleep at the park? _____

Answer Key

Lesson 1

Page 19
Sentence Comprehension
1. F
2. F
3. T
4. T
5. F

Word Study
I thought it would leap from my body.

Page 20
Paragraph Comprehension
1. c
2. a
3. a
4. c
5. c

Page 22
Whole Story Comprehension
1. a
2. c
3. d
4. a
5. b
6. a
7. a
8. b

Page 23
Enrichment
Answers will vary.

Page 24
Graphic Development
1. F
2. T
3. T
4. T
5. F

Lesson 2

Page 25
Sentence Comprehension
1. F
2. T
3. F
4. F
5. F

Word Study
Answers will vary.

Page 26
Paragraph Comprehension
1. a
2. b
3. d
4. d
5. a

Page 28
Whole Story Comprehension
1. c
2. b
3. a
4. a
5. c
6. d
7. b
8. d

Page 29
Enrichment
1. disappointment or surprise
2. excitement
3. amazement or excitement
4. amazement or excitement
5. excitement

Page 30
Graphic Development
1. leaf
2. blossom
3. stem
4. fruit
5. root

Lesson 3

Page 31
Sentence Comprehension
1. T
2. T
3. F
4. T
5. F

Word Study
shaman

Page 32
Paragraph Comprehension
1. a
2. b
3. d
4. c
5. a

Page 34
Whole Story Comprehension
1. d
2. b
3. c
4. b
5. d
6. c
7. c
8. b

Page 35
Enrichment
1. medicine man/doctor
2. writer
3. illustrator
4. pupil/apprentice/learner
5. town

Page 36
Graphic Development
1. F
2. T
3. T
4. F
5. T

Lesson 4

Page 37
Sentence Comprehension
1. F
2. T
3. T
4. T
5. T

Word Study
Answers will vary.

Page 38
Paragraph Comprehension
1. a
2. c
3. c
4. b
5. d

Page 40
Whole Story Comprehension
1. c
2. d
3. b
4. a
5. c
6. d
7. c
8. c

Page 41
Enrichment
1. 200
2. one
3. 25
4. eight
5. two
6. 60

Page 42
Graphic Development
1. arms
2. fins
3. head
4. eyes
5. mantle
6. funnel
7. tentacles

Answer Key *(cont.)*

Lesson 5

Page 43
Sentence Comprehension
1. T
2. F
3. F
4. T
5. T

Word Study
1. T
2. F
3. F
4. T
5. T

Page 44
Paragraph Comprehension
1. c
2. b
3. a
4. c
5. a

Page 46
Whole Story Comprehension
1. a
2. d
3. c
4. b
5. c
6. a
7. b
8. a

Page 47
Enrichment

gas: fuel that enables a car to function

gas: an element of the sun

Page 48
Graphic Development
1. yes
2. the top part
3. the bottom part

Lesson 6

Page 49
Sentence Comprehension
1. T
2. F
3. T
4. T
5. T

Word Study

reptile

Answers will vary.

Page 50
Paragraph Comprehension
1. a
2. c
3. a
4. d
5. d

Page 52
Whole Story Comprehension
1. c
2. a
3. c
4. a
5. c
6. b
7. c
8. c

Page 53
Enrichment

Answers will vary.

Page 54
Graphic Development
Dinosaur name: titanosaurs
How they looked: long necks; babies 15 inches long; adults over 50 feet
What they ate: plants
Where they were found: Argentina
What scientists found: eggs

Lesson 7

Page 55
Sentence Comprehension
1. F
2. T
3. T
4. F
5. T

Word Study

Endurance meant the ship could survive difficult situations.

Page 56
Paragraph Comprehension
1. c
2. b
3. a
4. a
5. b

Page 58
Whole Story Comprehension
1. d
2. c
3. a
4. c
5. b
6. b
7. b
8. d

Page 59
Enrichment
1. survive
2. drifted
3. stranded
4. rescue
5. endure

Page 60
Graphic Development
1. T
2. T
3. F
4. T
5. F

Lesson 8

Page 61
Sentence Comprehension
1. F
2. T
3. T
4. F
5. T

Word Study

There would be no more of some kinds of sharks left alive.

Page 62
Paragraph Comprehension
1. c
2. a
3. c
4. a
5. b

Page 64
Whole Story Comprehension
1. c
2. a
3. b
4. a
5. a
6. c
7. d
8. c

Page 65
Enrichment

Answers will vary.

Page 66
Graphic Development
1. caudal fin
2. gill slits
3. dorsal fins
4. pelvic fin
5. two

Answer Key (cont.)

Lesson 9

Page 67

Sentence Comprehension

1. F
2. T
3. T
4. T
5. T

Word Study

1. A
2. B
3. B
4. A

Page 68

Paragraph Comprehension

1. a
2. b
3. c
4. b
5. a

Page 70

Whole Story Comprehension

1. b
2. b
3. c
4. c
5. b
6. b
7. a
8. d

Page 71

Enrichment

1. "What time do we need to leave?" asked Kelly.
2. Gina said, "We really need to invite Jimmy."
3. "Do you think he'll want to go?" asked Mike.
4. "I think he will," said Leah.
5. They all said, "Okay, let's give him a call."
6.-8. Answers will vary.

Page 72

Graphic Development

1. Indian Ocean
2. east
3. Ethiopia
4. Somalia
5. west

Lesson 10

Page 73

Sentence Comprehension

1. T
2. F
3. T
4. T

Word Study

Answers will vary.

Page 74

Paragraph Comprehension

1. a
2. a
3. c
4. c
5. a

Page 76

Whole Story Comprehension

1. a
2. c
3. c
4. a
5. b
6. a
7. d
8. d

Page 77

Enrichment

1. would not
2. he is
3. who is
4. we are
5. you have
6. she will

Page 78

Graphic Development

Answers will vary.

Lesson 11

Page 79

Sentence Comprehension

1. F
2. T
3. T
4. T
5. F

Word Study

2. The astronauts landed on the moon.
3. The Apollo missions were trips to the moon.
4. *Prospector* will take pictures of the moon.

Page 80

Paragraph Comprehension

1. a
2. c
3. d
4. d
5. b

Page 82

Whole Story Comprehension

1. b
2. a
3. b
4. c
5. c
6. d
7. c
8. a

Page 83

Enrichment

1. spaceship
2. hallway
3. schoolhouse
4. notebook
5. sunrise
6. rainbow
7–10. Answers will vary.

Page 84

Graphic Development

1. F
2. T
3. T
4. F
5. T

Lesson 12

Page 85

Sentence Comprehension

1. T
2. F
3. T
4. F
5. F

Word Study

1. firefighter
2. homework
3. crime
4. emergency
5. safe

Page 86

Paragraph Comprehension

1. b
2. a
3. d
4. c
5. c

Page 88

Whole Story Comprehension

1. a
2. c
3. a
4. c
5. c
6. c
7. a
8. c

Answer Key (cont.)

Page 89
Enrichment
1. fire fighter
2. base ball
3. basket ball
4. foot ball
5. home work
6. bath room
7.-10. Answers will vary

Page 90
Graphic Development
Problem: Engine Company 16 was a place for crime

What did they do? stopped locking the building

Who came to visit? kids (during school)

How did the firefighters help the kids? They encouraged school attendance with prizes; they taught them chess; cut hair; help with homework; collect clothes

What do kids and firefighters do together? Play sports

Lesson 13

Page 91
Sentence Comprehension
1. F
2. F
3. T
4. T
5. T
Word Study
1. estuary
2. marsh
3. marsh
4. estuary

Page 92
Paragraph Comprehension
1. a
2. d
3. c
4. a
5. d

Page 94
Whole Story Comprehension
1. c
2. b
3. a
4. d
5. a
6. c
7. c
8. a

Page 95
Enrichment
Answers will vary.

Page 96
Graphic Development

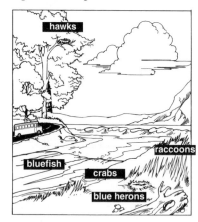

Lesson 14

Page 97
Sentence Comprehension
1. F
2. T
3. T
4. F
5. F
Word Study
Answers will vary.

Page 98
Paragraph Comprehension
1. c
2. a
3. d
4. a
5. b

Page 100
Whole Story Comprehension
1. b
2. a
3. c
4. c
5. a
6. b
7. a
8. b

Page 101
Enrichment
1. Jupiter
2. system
3. Saturn
4. discovery
5.–8. Answers will vary.

Lesson 15

Page 102
Graphic Development
Answers will vary.

Page 103
Sentence Comprehension
1. T
2. T
3. F
4. T
5. F
Word Study
1. F
2. O
3. O
4. F
5. O
6. O

Page 104
Paragraph Comprehension
1. c
2. d
3. a
4. a
5. b

Page 106
Whole Story Comprehension
1. b
2. b
3. d
4. c
5. d
6. a
7. b
8. c

Page 107
Enrichment
Answers will vary.

Page 108
Graphic Development
Answers will vary.

Lesson 16

Page 109
Sentence Comprehension
1. T
2. T
3. F
4. T
Word Study
Healthy: fruit, chicken, milk, salad
Not-So-Healthy: chips, candy, French fries, soda pop

Page 110
Paragraph Comprehension
1. b
2. a
3. a
4. c
5. c

Answer Key (cont.)

Page 112
Whole Story Comprehension
1. b
2. b
3. a
4. b
5. c
6. a
7. b
8. a

Page 113
Enrichment
Answers will vary.

Page 114
Graphic Development
Answers will vary.

Lesson 17

Page 115
Sentence Comprehension
1. T
2. T
3. F
4. T
5. T
Word Study
Answers will vary.

Page 116
Paragraph Comprehension
1. b
2. c
3. a
4. a
5. c

Page 118
Whole Story Comprehension
1. d
2. b
3. a
4. d
5. a
6. b
7. d
8. a

Page 119
Enrichment
Answers will vary.

Page 120
Graphic Development
1. about 27%
2. 1997
3. less
4. Answers will vary.

Lesson 18

Page 121
Sentence Comprehension
1. T
2. T
3. F
4. T
5. T
Word Study
Answers will vary.

Page 122
Paragraph Comprehension
1. c
2. a
3. c
4. c
5. a

Page 124
Whole Story Comprehension
1. d
2. d
3. a
4. b
5. a
6. c
7. b
8. a

Page 125
Enrichment
1. People, villages, and animals are near the river.
2. The dam will stop flooding, keep people safe, and make electricity.
3. Building a dam takes time, hard work, and money.
4. More electricity will help people, businesses, and towns.

Page 126
Graphic Development
1. Kunlun Mountains
2. Shanghai
3. East China Sea
4. Kunming, Chengdu, Chongqing, Wuhan, Nanjing, Shanghai

Lesson 19

Page 127
Sentence Comprehension
1. T
2. F
3. T
4. T
Word Study
Answers will vary.

Page 128
Paragraph Comprehension
1. d
2. c
3. c
4. c
5. a

Page 130
Whole Story Comprehension
1. a
2. c
3. c
4. a
5. c
6. b
7. c
8. d

Page 131
Enrichment
Answers will vary.

Page 132
Graphic Development
1. Mt. Kailash and Mt. Everest
2. seven
3. Sakya
4. Lhasa

Lesson 20

Page 133
Sentence Comprehension
1. F
2. T
3. F
4. F
5. T
Word Study
Answers will vary.

Page 134
Paragraph Comprehension
1. d
2. c
3. a
4. b
5. c

Page 136
Whole Story Comprehension
1. c   5. a
2. a   6. a
3. c   7. b
4. c   8. a

Page 137
Enrichment
Answers will vary.

Page 138
Graphic Development
1. campground
2. picnic area
3. boat
4. horse
5. store
6. camp, have a picnic, ride horses, go boating, shop
7. at a campground (also accept lodge or cabins)

Answer Sheet

Directions: Fill in the bubble of the correct answer "a," "b," "c," "d," or "e" on this sheet. If the answer is "True," fill in the "a" bubble, and if the answer is "False," fill in the "b" bubble.

T F   T F   T F   T F

(The sheet consists of four columns of answer bubbles labeled (a) (b) (c) (d) (e), with a blank line preceding each row for the question number.)